W9-CKR-895

THE
OHIO STATE BUCKEYES FANS'
BUCKET LIST

THE
OHIO STATE BUCKEYES FANS'
BUCKET LIST

ZACK MEISEL

TRIUMPH
BOOKS

Library of Congress Cataloging-in-Publication Data

Meisel, Zack, 1989–
    The Ohio State Buckeyes fans' bucket list / Zack Meisel.
        pages cm. — (Bucket list)
    ISBN 978-1-62937-157-3 (paperback)
    1. Ohio State University—Sports—Miscellanea. I. Title.
    GV691.O4M45 2015
    796.04'30977156—dc23
                                        2015015304

This book is available in quantity at special discounts for your group or organization. For further information, contact:

Triumph Books LLC
814 North Franklin Street
Chicago, Illinois 60610
(312) 337-0747
www.triumphbooks.com

Printed in U.S.A.
ISBN: 978-1-62937-157-3
Design by Andy Hansen
Page Production by Patricia Frey

Photos: Gottesman Photography

For my sister, Veronica, who deserves recognition for her support, despite never replacing my sunglasses, which she tossed to the bottom of Lake Lanier.

And for Laurel, who has put up with my late nights of writing that occasionally culminate in a loud thud as I, half-asleep, walk into a closed door. Her support and motivation were a driving force behind this book and much more. I'll never forget the first time she saw Ohio Stadium, which could hold about 50 times the student population of her alma mater, Allegheny College.

Contents

Introduction

There is a trail alongside the Olentangy River that weaves through the west side of Ohio State's campus. It meanders past Ohio Stadium and Lincoln and Morrill Towers, dips below Lane Avenue, and wanders through Tuttle Park and beyond. It is frequented by joggers, walkers, runners, and bench-sitters.

It is a path I have traveled often, a path quiet and serene enough to permit deep thinking. The first time I navigated the trail, as I passed The Shoe, I reflected upon my first visit to the venue in 2008. The Buckeyes—ranked No. 9—were hosting No. 3 Penn State for a nationally televised night game. I had been handed my credential for *The Lantern*, the school newspaper, days in advance. When Saturday arrived, I was a wreck. I had attended football games with 70,000 others. But here I was, a 19-year-old kid with no experience in game coverage, tasked with writing about an affair played before 105,000 people. That was too much pressure. So I opted not to go. Who cares? I will never show my face again in *The Lantern* newsroom. I will ignore every text and call from the sports editor. I will find a new career field. I just could not confront those jitters.

The standards associated with Ohio State football are a gift and a curse for the writers. Anything short of an undefeated season and a national championship can, in some light, be considered a disappointment. Every game carries immeasurable implications. Every misstep could cost the Buckeyes a season's worth of hope and optimism and expectation. For the writers, that creates plenty of pressure. Every key play and result requires an appropriate level of description and perspective. For those not accustomed to such a degree of tension, it can be intimidating.

I did not want to face that fear. So I sat in my dorm room, staring at my laptop, my leg shaking uncontrollably, my teeth chewing apart whichever fingernail was next. Finally, I decided to walk over to the stadium. I stepped into the press box and peered out at the stands, filled with fans in scarlet. Words cannot do it justice. The roar of the crowd when the Buckeyes stormed the field cannot be described with some lazy choice of onomatopoeia.

I did not have to be convinced again. I did not have to think twice about honoring my duties at Ohio Stadium. Ohio State lost that evening, but I was hooked. I fed off the pressure. The unrelenting energy created by the capacity crowd fueled me with adrenaline. The stress was fun. The early September contest against an overmatched MAC opponent that makes the trek to Columbus primarily for a chance to collect a paycheck? Those are the tough games to cover. Those require more use of the creative part of the brain. The games against Michigan or Michigan State that carry with them a ticket to the Big Ten Championship Game? The events that unfold within those 60 minutes of football often write themselves. Those moments are easier, more enjoyable, and more rewarding to chronicle. The stakes are higher. The crowd is louder. More eyes are watching. I grew to love to embrace that pressure.

I would traverse that trail almost daily, without a care in the world. Aside from the occasional clicking of a bicycle chain or the chirping of a few birds, the path was silent. No noise, no stirring, no pressure. Sometimes, when I would see the Block "O" that adorns the top of the south stands peeking out above a cluster of trees, I would reminisce about that night, when I almost bypassed my first—and, perhaps, only, if not for my ultimate decision—chance at covering the perennial national championship contender. As soon as I was asked to write this book, that rush returned. Deadlines offered pressure. Interviews and late nights spent writing provided heaps of stress. I would not want it any other way.

Chapter 1

Coaching Stories

Woody Hayes' old cabin sits up a hill in a wooded area in the small, rural town of Caldwell, Ohio.

Visit Woody Hayes' Cabin

Ten miles. Ten twisting miles winding down a wayward path devoid of visibility, with nary a streetlight nor stop sign to impede. The sights along the route are antiquated and unconventional, rural and unsophisticated. A collection of rusty, downtrodden cars, the ignitions long untapped, rest among weeds and tall, untamed grass. A tire covers the hood of a navy sedan parked in front of a patch of woods. A ceramics shop, a bar, and an inn sit atop dirt lots at various junctures along the trail. Farms line both sides of the road, with cows and horses roaming the giant pastures that keep plenty of distance between neighbors.

Ten miles of this, before ultimately reaching the hidden gem of Caldwell, Ohio. Ten miles to Woody Hayes' old cabin.

The pathway is easy to overlook. It peeks out just before a sharp left turn on the main road. The rusty gate, innocent yet inviting, hangs ajar, but blends in with the backdrop of leaves, trees, and earth. Up the steep hill lies the log fixture, sold multiple times since Woody died in 1987. The cabin and the quirky town surrounding it are where Woody rushed to escape from football, from work, and from life; where he reconnected with his extended family; where he chatted about school and jobs with the 12 children of Mary Hill, a widowed neighbor.

This, in essence, was home.

"He never forgot to come back," said Mabel Schott, Woody's second cousin.

No one in town had seen Woody Hayes since he punched that player and lost his job. Everyone was on the same page, though. No one wanted to prompt that uncomfortable conversation.

Gennie Saling knew her husband. She knew all too well of the lack of a filter between his brain and his mouth. So, Gennie warned Ed.

"Don't you say anything to him about that," she told him.

Woody always stopped by the Saling residence on his visits to Caldwell. Upon his arrival, the words flowed from Ed's mouth with reckless abandon. He approached Woody and asked: "What the hell can make a man do that?" Gennie shook her head. Of course he asked about it.

On Saturday afternoons during the summer, Woody walked up the street to the bar owned by his cousin and bought everyone drinks. Woody knew every patron at the three bars in town. Everyone in Caldwell knew Woody. Of course, unfamiliarity does not really exist in the small community.

"Everybody knows everybody and everybody knows everybody's business," said Schott, whose white front door bears an Ohio State adornment.

In Columbus, where he coached for 28 years, Woody was a daunting, directive dictator. Former Ohio State coach Earle Bruce, who succeeded Woody as the Buckeyes' boss, said Woody almost always drove places by himself. "But if he rode with you, it was his car and he took over the radio, took over the windows, took over the heat. He took over everything. He was always in control."

In reality, though, Woody was a recluse.

"He used to go mountain hiking all the time by himself," Bruce said. "He was always kind of a loner in that respect."

In Caldwell, Woody was a hallowed figure, revered for his five national championships but respected and beloved for his generosity. He stood out, sure, but at the same time, he fit in seamlessly with the small town's people.

"It was the complete opposite," said Melinda Antill, one of eight Saling children. "Nobody was intimidated by Woody Hayes around here."

Woody visited on weekends during the summer. In the winter, snow and ice blanketed the steep gravel path to his cabin, creating a nearly impossible trail to traverse. When he returned to Caldwell, he steered the conversation away from his own legacy.

"Never once did that man ever talk football," Gennie Saling said. "All he ever talked about was learning and working."

Once a year, Woody provided a set of tickets to the denizens of Caldwell. They filled a car or two and made the two-hour trek west to Columbus and sat in the front row to watch their hero lead Ohio State.

"My kids, they used to go to school and tell people they met Woody Hayes," Saling said. "Kids didn't want to believe them."

Here was this man, this imposing figure, the stirring face of one of college football's premier programs, a seemingly callous coach who was ultimately dismissed for striking an opposing player. Yet in Caldwell, where he spent his childhood summers on his grandparents' farm and his offseason weekends in his secluded log cabin, Woody conformed to a simple, innocent manner of life.

"I liked to talk to him," Schott said. "He was really understanding. He liked everybody."

No one appreciated Gennie Saling's work ethic more than Woody did. She plucked worms off of the tobacco on her family's farm and she threw the burrowing bodies into a can. She milked cows, tended to horses, did housework for neighbors, served at all three bars in town, and worked at a steel plant. She could operate every machine in that factory. Woody admired that.

He stopped in at the Saling residence on Sundays. He would bring a case of beer for the adults and a watermelon for everyone else and he would sit in a chair in the living room and preach about the value of education to the family's children, grandchildren, and the rest of the kids in the neighborhood. They had all heard tales about Woody making his players stay at his house under his watchful eye until they improved their grades.

"I was told that if they weren't making their grades, you did not want a teacher giving him a phone call," Antill said. "If he got a phone call, you were dead meat."

So, Woody spoke to the roomful of children each week and relayed the importance of studying and completing homework.

"He always told them: 'Get an education first,'"Antill said. "'It's not all about football. You have to have the education or the football ain't gonna get you nowhere.'"

In the early 1940s, Gennie—then 17—married Ed, who worked for a local coal company that tore down old houses, which were really just log structures with siding. Ed had taken the logs and built two cabins on his farm. They caught Woody's eye.

Woody secured an acre of land atop a majestic hill and he hired Ed and Joe Schott—Mabel's husband—to build him a new abode. Years later, the complex still sits on the same grounds. The exterior looks like a faded American flag or a dual-flavored birthday cake. Layers of white- and brown-stained wood compose the framework. A cluster of barren wasp nests hangs from the track of the front door. Two wooden benches rest on the porch, one of them sporting a busted leg that prohibits any sitting. Woody often settled onto one of the seats and read or wrote. He penned a book about football, which Antill keeps in her home. He would read about world history and famous battles and anything that Ralph Waldo Emerson composed. The stone chimney started to reluctantly separate from the foundation of the cabin, as the old mortar in between pleads for its life. In the spring, Easter lilies blossom all throughout the surrounding woods. Antill says they spring up "everywhere" one looks.

Woody installed a red sink and a gray bathtub to give the place Ohio State flair. He had an Ohio State rug near the front door. Long after his passing, a grill and a Jacuzzi were added outside of the cabin. The grass was littered with empty cans of Natty Light.

A large yellow candle, two smaller, exhausted candles, a book, a white porcelain bowl, and a picture frame rest on a wooden table in the center of the cabin. A blanket is draped over the back of one of four chairs positioned around the table. A tall, rustic lamp hovers over a leather chair. White curtains, decorated with a blue floral design, shield the inside from too much sunlight. The lodge boasts a fireplace, a living room, a kitchen, a bathroom, and a bedroom loft.

The Salings used to tend to the cabin when Woody was away. Gennie mowed the lawn and even did Woody's laundry. He called her to say he was coming to town and he would stop by to exchange his dirty clothes for his clean garb. When Woody died, Gennie still had his clothes hanging upstairs. Now, her grandson has Woody's patented button-up short-sleeve shirt framed in glass hanging on a wall in his house. Caldwell is home to several branches of the Hayes family tree,

EXTRA POINTS

"I'm not resigning!"

The tension in the room was palpable. No one wanted to utter a word, out of fear of how Woody Hayes might respond. Ohio State lost to Michigan 7–0 to cap Woody's first season as head coach in Columbus. The Buckeyes finished the 1951 campaign with an underwhelming 4–3–2 record. Underwhelming by Woody's standards, especially. After the loss in Ann Arbor, Michigan, Woody called a meeting at his house. In the living room sat Bo Schembechler, a 22-year-old graduate assistant, along with the rest of the coaching staff. Woody was using a projector with 16-millimeter film to analyze what went wrong at Michigan Stadium.

"He's running it back and forth," Schembechler said. "I'm sitting in the back of the room, staying out of the way, and he's getting madder and madder. And suddenly, he picked up that projector and threw it."

Woody shouted: "I won't subject the people of Columbus to football like that!"

"I'll never forget him saying that," Schembechler said.

Early on in the following week, assistant coach Ernie Godfrey entered a staff meeting and said: "Woody, the people downtown who have the jobs are pulling the jobs out. We're going to lose most of our jobs downtown."

"Back then, you work for your room and board and stuff," Schembechler said. "I'll never forget, Woody said: 'Well, now, they wouldn't take the jobs away if I resigned, would they?'"

"No, they wouldn't," Godfrey replied.

"Well, you tell them," Woody said, "God damn, I'll pay the players myself. I'll mortgage the damn house. I'll borrow the money. I'll pay them myself. But I'm not resigning!"

Three years later, Woody directed Ohio State to a national championship with an unblemished 10–0 record, including a Rose Bowl victory against USC.

"He was a tough son of a gun," Schembechler said. "You don't run him out of town that easily."

but even to those in the area not related by blood, Woody was like family.

"He was in this house and this kitchen more times than I can count," Antill said.

One time, his visit made Gennie nervous. Woody was bringing his wife to town for the first time. Caldwell did not—and does not—attract many visitors. Butch and Patti Damewood relocated to the area from Akron, Ohio, just for that purpose. They built a home on the main road and purchased the vacant property next door—the land adjacent to Woody's old estate—so they could maintain solitude and privacy. They sit at their kitchen table, catch up on news, and let their robotic vacuum cleaner tidy up the house.

Despite his ability to ease into the town's structure, Woody was still a superstar in Caldwell. Many who grow up in the area spend their entire lives there. Woody, meanwhile, coached a national spectacle of a football team that occasionally played in front of crowds the size of 50 times the population of Caldwell. Gennie envisioned Woody's wife as a high-class, hoity-toity, elegant, posh woman to whom she would not be able to relate. Then, Anne stepped out of the car.

"Here she comes, this little old heavy-set lady who had her hair back in a bunch like a farm lady," Saling said. "She was just like a farm lady, too. She was the nicest person that you could meet."

They hit it off. Once Woody died, Anne mailed Gennie $100 each Christmas. Anne died in 1998.

The Salings shared a special bond with Woody. He was not the same person in Caldwell—where he was alone and at peace in his cabin or at the bar or in a neighbor's living room before a cluster of kids—as he was in Columbus. There, he was obsessed with his work and rooted in his tunnel vision. His team and the responsibility associated with his job occupied every instant of his daily life.

"He was a very good-hearted person," Antill said. "It was amazing how good he could be to people. If anyone needed something, he would definitely help you."

Because of that, Ed Saling could not believe what Woody did during the waning moments of the 1978 Gator Bowl against Clemson. Woody punched Charlie Bauman, a defensive player on Clemson who had intercepted a pass. He was later fired for his action. Ed and Woody never shied away from speaking their minds to each other, though.

So, Ed asked: "What the hell can make a man do that?"

Woody replied: "They ticked me off!"

That was the end of the conversation.

"You'd just have to know Woody," Antill said. "He had a temper. There's no doubt about that."

They knew Woody in Caldwell, and maybe a little better than most.

. . . .

Honor Woody's Legacy

What is Woody Hayes' legacy at Ohio State? Just look around the campus.

Beginning near Ohio Stadium and venturing west is Woody Hayes Drive. Woody's Tavern serves pizza, beer, wine, popcorn, and root beer in the student union. Football players and coaches spend hours each day of the year in the Woody Hayes Athletic Center, a sports complex with practice fields that sit a short walk from the Schottenstein Center.

The longtime coach's presence on the campus should come as no surprise. In his 28 seasons at the helm for the Buckeyes, he compiled a 205–61–10 record, including a 152–37–7 mark in Big Ten play. Under Hayes, Ohio State was a recruiting powerhouse, a machine that churned out nine- and 10-win seasons and annually vied for national titles. During his reign, they captured five national championships and 13 of the conference variety. Woody was twice pegged as the Big Ten Coach of the Year and three times as the College Football Coach of the Year. He directed the Buckeyes to eight Rose Bowls, of which they won four. On four occasions (1954, 1961, 1968, 1973), his Ohio State teams went the entire season without a defeat.

Woody sprouted a coaching tree that produced branches upon branches full of future college or professional football hires. Those who studied under Hayes included Earle Bruce, Lou Holtz, Ara Parseghian, and Bo Schembechler.

The wrinkle of Woody's personality that stands out most, however, might be his ruthlessness. He demanded the best out of everyone he encountered, be it his players, the media covering his team, or the students taking his military history course in Converse Hall.

The sultan of Ohio State football would periodically check on his players after dark to ensure they were studying. So one night when Rudy Hubbard hosted a poker game in his dorm room with a few teammates and a couple of nonplayers who smoked cigarettes, the telling taps on the door shook the tailback to his core.

He knew those knuckles belonged to Woody, and the coach tossed everyone out of the room. Everyone but Hubbard. After heaving an ashtray at the wall, he sat Hubbard down and told him that if any other authority had caught him pulling this garbage, he would have been dismissed from the team.

"He could have you scared to death and at the same time make you love him for the fact that he cared about you," Hubbard said. "I just saw that as Woody being Woody."

Over time, Hubbard and Woody developed a bond, one no one would have thought possible once Hubbard arrived at Ohio State in 1964 with aspirations to play professional football like his idol, Jim Brown. Hubbard, though, spent most of his time blocking for Jim Otis, Paul Hudson, or Bo Rein. In his final game in 1967, a 24–14 win at Michigan, he rushed for 103 yards and two touchdowns, matching his career total. The performance validated what he had thought all along, that he could excel as the focal point of an offense. After the game, assistant coach Larry Catuzzi, aware of Rudy's frustration, asked him: "You're glad to be leaving here, right?"

Hubbard's high school held a banquet that winter to honor his college achievements. Hubbard stood before friends, family, and former classmates and delivered a rant fueled by the animosity that flowed through his veins for four years as he watched Ohio State's quarterbacks hand the ball elsewhere.

"I was disenchanted," Hubbard said. "I thought I would have a much better career than what I had."

Woody was in attendance, but Hubbard didn't care. He figured he would never again see his old coach, since his eligibility had expired. When Woody called him a few weeks later and set up an appointment to meet with him, Hubbard figured his old coach planned to admonish him for his heated remarks at the reception.

Instead, Woody offered Hubbard the opportunity to be the first African American football coach at Ohio State. Hubbard was blown away. Despite being drafted by the Montreal Alouettes of the Canadian Football League, Hubbard accepted the bullish coach's offer. Perhaps Woody actually appreciated Hubbard's candid tirade.

"[Hubbard] was not afraid to speak his mind," said former Ohio State running back Archie Griffin. "He never has been. I think Coach Hayes respected that about Rudy."

Woody was stubborn and rooted in his ways. He told his coaches that if everyone kept driving cars, there would be an energy crisis. So he

THE DECISION

Bo Schembechler liked to tell the story of when Woody Hayes had to accept not being in control. Ohio State had thumped Michigan 50–20 in Ann Arbor in the last week of November 1961. The win pushed the Buckeyes to 8–0–1 and 6–0 in the Big Ten, which secured them the conference title and would have earned them a Rose Bowl bid. Only, the Ohio State faculty voted that the team would not play in the Rose Bowl—and have a shot at the national championship—and would instead emphasize academics above athletics.

Hayes and Schembechler, then his assistant coach, were at an alumni dinner in Cleveland when the faculty relayed the message to Woody.

"That was something else," Schembechler said. "And so Woody said, 'Get your coat.' So I got my coat."

The banquet was filled to capacity with alumni celebrating the lopsided victory over Michigan and the undefeated season. But Woody needed to leave, needed to let off some steam and stew for a bit. He and Schembechler strolled through the streets of Cleveland until about 9:00 PM. For parts of the journey, the two coaches talked. Other parts of the trek were spent in uncomfortable silence. Finally, the two retreated to the hotel that was hosting the reception. Woody took the stage and delivered what Schembechler described as "one of the great speeches you ever heard."

The lengthy walk had allowed Woody to simmer a bit. Instead of standing at the podium and offering a profanity-laced tirade, he merely orated that the faculty has a right to form their own opinion. Of course, he could not refrain from mentioning "how dastardly wrong it is," Schembechler recalled. Woody claimed it was a result of university politics and stressed that no one cared to consider how hard players and staff members worked to plod their way through an unbeaten season.

The Big Ten had a no-repeat rule for the Rose Bowl until 1972, a mandate that stated no team from the conference could participate in the bowl game in consecutive years. Minnesota had played in the Rose Bowl the year before, but since Ohio State declined its invitation, the Golden Gophers returned to Pasadena, California. Certainly, the university decision makers could not have expected Woody to quietly accept that choice.

"I'll never forget that," Schembechler said.

walked to work. By the time the team wrapped up practice, Woody was too exhausted to hoof it back home. So, he routinely asked Hubbard for a ride home, only he would make him take a detour and stop for a pecan roll and subsequently spend all night chatting with his assistant.

"He dominated the conversation most of the time," Hubbard said. "Most people ended up doing whatever he wanted them to."

That applied to his recruits, as well.

"He's the best recruiter, maybe in the history of sports," said former quarterback Bill Long. "He got so personal, with not only the athletes, but the families."

And in the end, he typically got what he wanted. He attended a basketball game with Long and Long's parents during the process of recruiting Long to Ohio State. Long did not want to commit to the school that night. He had never been on an airplane. He loved the idea of traveling across the country, schmoozing with suitors who sought his services. He hoped to fly to Wisconsin and Colorado. He planned to visit Northwestern. He wanted to milk the process the best he could.

At halftime of the basketball game, Woody brought Long to his office. The two sat down at the coach's desk and Woody pulled out a vocabulary book.

"OK, Bill," he said. "I'm going to go over some words with you right now."

Long was a bit confused. What did vocabulary have to do with anything?

"Adjacent," Woody said. "Spell *adjacent*."

Long supplied the "A" and the "D" before he stumbled. Woody cut him off and corrected him.

"No, god dammit," Woody said. "That's not right. It's 'A-D-J.' You should know by now, Bill. Now, give me the definition of adjacent."

Long, still perplexed, offered a response.

"Now use it in a sentence," Woody demanded.

This sequence persisted for the entire second half of the basketball game. Finally, the coach closed the book and shot straight.

"OK, let's get down to business," Woody said. "I know you want to come to Ohio State. Let's get this over with and commit tonight."

Long hesitated. He told Woody that he was "95 percent sure" he wanted to attend Ohio State, but that he would prefer to wait before he secured his decision. Woody seemed to accept that answer and the two rejoined Long's parents.

"I felt like I beat him," Long said. "I was walking on air."

Ah, but Woody was such a pro. He had his recruit right where he wanted him. The four went out for dinner at a restaurant down the street. Woody spotted Ritter Collett, a writer and editor for the Dayton *Journal-Herald*.

"Ritter, you know Bob Long and his wife, Shorty," Woody said. "We're recruiting their son, Bill Long. Ritter, Bill has something to tell you."

Long's eyes opened wide. His jaw might as well have been resting on the floor. Woody got him. So sly, so shrewd, so calculated. How did he do it?

"Yeah," Long said. "I've decided to come to Ohio State."

Long did not come to regret that decision. He appreciated Woody's involvement in the recruiting process.

"At all of the other schools, assistants did everything," Long said. "You only saw the head coach right before you went home. They were just above it. But not Woody."

Long had planned to major in art. At one point before Long officially enrolled, Woody summoned the high school senior to his office and asked him to bring some of his artwork. Woody picked up the phone on his desk and called Ohio State's fine arts department.

"I want a meeting with one of your people over there," he said. "I have a recruit who is interested in art and I want you to take a look at his work."

Long could not believe how invested Woody chose to get with his prospective players. In turn, that earned Woody unparalleled respect. His players respected him to the point of fear. Hubbard thought he knew Woody as well as anybody did. So, when anyone needed to consult Woody about something, they typically enlisted Hubbard's help.

"We were all scared of him," Hubbard said. "I wasn't any different. There were times when I'd go talk to him and my nerves were up and I'd go in there and leave and didn't get a thing done."

Woody died from a heart attack in 1987. Hubbard had two decades to ask why Woody offered him that coaching position, but he never did.

Controversy often followed Woody wherever he went. He was involved in scuffles with sportswriters and cameramen and athletic directors. He ran up the score against rival Michigan, as his Buckeyes attempted a two-point conversion while commanding a 50–14 lead in 1968. Legend has it that he proclaimed after the affair that he opted to go for two because he "couldn't go for three." His captaincy infamously ended when he struck a Clemson player in the Gator Bowl a decade later.

Still, Woody remains revered in Columbus. There exists plenty of evidence around campus to support as much.

. . . .

Hear the Marching Band Play "Hang on Sloopy"

John Tatgenhorst handed Charles Spohn a cassette. On the tape was the tune to The McCoys' hit song, "Hang on Sloopy." Tatgenhorst had created his own version, set to the key of G-flat, for Ohio State's Marching Band. Spohn gave it a listen.

"The Ohio State Marching Band will not play that kind of stuff," Spohn told Tatgenhorst that day in 1965.

Only, he did not say the word *stuff*.

"It was a different word that starts with the 'S,'" Tatgenhorst recalled a half-century later.

Weeks passed. After Tatgenhorst's barrage of begging and pleading, Spohn finally caved.

"Go ahead and arrange the son of a gun," the band director said to his musical arranger.

Only, he did not say the word *gun*.

On September 13, 2014, the university honored Tatgenhorst for his 50 years of service to the marching band at the Skull Session, a Saturday staple on Ohio State's campus during football season.

"There is one arrangement that has guaranteed your immortality in Buckeye lore," said the band director as he introduced Tatgenhorst to the raucous crowd at St. John Arena. "Back in 1965, director Charles Spohn allowed you to arrange a popular rock song by a group known as The McCoys and the tradition was born."

Tatgenhorst was a percussion student at Ohio State. In 1964, he replaced Richard Heine as the musical arranger for the OSU Marching Band. He was responsible for identifying rock and roll hits and pop songs for the band to play. Tatgenhorst was playing drums for Channel 4 TV at a live promote at the Ohio State Fair that summer when he heard "Hang on Sloopy" over the event's PA system.

"I have a way, when I hear something, I have to hear the band playing it," Tatgenhorst said. "Not just hearing the song, but the range and how it would be done."

He thought The McCoys' track would fit the profile for the band, so he presented the idea to Spohn. The boss was not having any of it. Tatgenhorst, though, refused to relent.

"I hounded Charlie every week or so," Tatgenhorst said. "I tested him constantly about this tune."

One Thursday evening, Tatgenhorst was teaching private classes to students at a music school. At about 7:00 PM—an hour and a half before his class was scheduled to end—Tatgenhorst received a phone call from Spohn, who told him to prepare "Hang on Sloopy" for the band's use. After class, Tatgenhorst completed the 30-minute trek to

The Ohio State Marching Band has played "Hang on Sloopy," by The McCoys, since 1965.

his residence. He grabbed something to eat and plopped himself down to start working at 9:30 PM.

"I had it in my ear what I wanted to do with it," said Tatgenhorst as he hummed the original tune.

He arranged the song in the key of "F" and after nearly four hours of work, he settled into bed a little after 1:00 AM. It was not right, though. That was not the most appropriate key.

"I said, 'Get your butt out of bed and modulate so it's more interesting,'" Tatgenhorst said.

So he switched everything to the key of G-flat and, blurry-eyed, he wrapped up his work after 2:00 AM. He could not finish everything, however, as he had to wake up early the next morning to play drums for Channel 4.

A week later, on October 9, 1965, Ohio State hosted Illinois at the Horseshoe. Rain plummeted from the cloud-covered sky all afternoon. Fans gripped umbrellas as the Buckeyes dispatched the Fighting Illini 28–14. The band was not allowed on the muddy field, so it played its lineup from the sideline. It performed "Hang on Sloopy," but received an apathetic response from the soggy crowd.

"I thought, *Oh, god. All of the fighting I've done for months and that's that,*" Tatgenhorst said.

At Ohio State's next home game, however, the band played the song again. This time, the fans bought in.

"It got a thunderous ovation," Tatgenhorst said.

Over time, the song became an entire production. Cheerleaders initiated the custom of forming the state's letters with their hands between each stanza of the chorus. Eventually, the band settled on the intermission between the third and fourth quarters to play the tune at each game. In 1985, "Hang on Sloopy" was designated as the state of Ohio's official rock song.

"Some things catch on and some things don't," Tatgenhorst said. "I never thought it would be a very, very important school song. Sometimes you just throw things up the flagpole and hope that they stick."

Tatgenhorst proceeded to compose music for a litany of TV shows, including "The Adventures of Batman & Robin," "Live with Regis and Kelly," and newscasts and advertisements for all of the major networks. He also directed music for the Indianapolis 500, the U.S. Marine Band, and various orchestras around the world. And after 50 years of arranging music for Ohio State's Marching Band, the university honored him with a tribute to his achievements, the chief one among them being his choice of "Hang on Sloopy." The band even spelled out "John T" on the field one game. They were a bit short on the manpower required to spell out his entire surname.

"I appreciated it very, very much," Tatgenhorst said. "Sloopy will outlast my lifetime. I appreciated the tribute they gave me on 50 years [as musical arranger]. I won't make it to 100."

. . . .

Woody and Urban: Two Peas in a Pod

A sly grin sweeps across Urban Meyer's face. He plays it off as though he has never heard the comparison. He has, though.

Meyer coached under Earle Bruce, who coached under Woody Hayes. Bruce sees the resemblance between his predecessor and his prodigy. So does Bruce's grandson, Zach Smith, who, under Meyer's direction, coaches Ohio State's receivers.

"He's somebody that loves Ohio State, that's competitive, intense," Smith said of Meyer, "and at the same time, deep down, cares about his players and assistant coaches."

That would describe Meyer, hired as Ohio State's head honcho near the end of the 2011 calendar year. It would also fit the description for Woody, who coached at Ohio State from 1951 to 1978.

"I see a lot of similarities between the two of them," said Ohio State football historian Jack Park. "They are honest to a fault, really."

Park noticed the resemblance when he listened to Meyer gripe about a lackluster effort put forth by his players during a spring practice, just two months after the Buckeyes captured the national championship. As soon as the coach said he would have serious talks with his players and coaches about the spring performance, Park thought of Woody. He reminisced about how Woody built a foundation in his early years at Ohio State. Quickly, he became the face of the football program, and his persona lured recruits to the university. All of it fueled a successful 28-year stint as head coach. Meyer has paved a parallel path.

"Meyer has laid out an environment for success and players have bought into it," Park said.

Meyer was an assistant at Ohio State from 1986 to 1987, less than a decade after Bruce replaced Woody as head coach in Columbus. To those familiar with both men, some of the similarities in style, demeanor, and authority are striking. After Ohio State won at California in September 2013, Jim Otis, a fullback for Woody's squad from 1967 to 1969, texted Meyer and relayed that message.

"He does have a little bit of Woody in him," Otis said. "He coached with Earle and Earle is a disciple of Woody's, so you're going to get a lot of Woody. There's a big difference between Earle and Woody, but Urban has that."

Woody was the emperor, the dictator no one wanted to tweak or disturb. He hired Rudy Hubbard to coach the running backs, but Woody actually preferred to preside over that position group. When Hubbard asked to design plays for the running backs, Woody replied, "Well, what do you think *I'm* going to do?"

"So I'm thinking, *Well, what did you hire me for, then?*" Hubbard said. "Shortly after that, he asked me to draw up plays and I came in early and got them all up and he was shocked. So after that, I never had a problem with that."

Bruce said Woody was always in control, on and off the field, while a passenger in someone else's car—he would command the air flow, the radio dial, and whether the windows were rolled down, completely shut, or something in between—or even while hiking up a mountain by himself.

"These guys were afraid to pick out a movie the night before a game," said former Ohio State quarterback Bill Long, "because Woody might not like the movie."

Meyer might not be a stickler when it comes to choosing between a horror flick and a romantic comedy. He might not appear as hardened or unreasonable. He does, though, have a comparable command for respect.

"This coach, you talk about this guy getting these guys ready. Jesus Christ," Long said. "These guys were playing hard all through a 56–0 game [against Purdue in 2013] and they didn't slow down. That's hard to coach. He has them thinking. This guy is something. To do that with modern kids, this guy has them almost playing scared, which is pretty interesting."

The coaches also share an obsessive commitment to their job. Meyer stepped down at Florida, escaping the mounting stress that took a toll on his health and his relationship with his family. After a year off, he relocated to Columbus, but only after he signed a contract devised by his daughters that mandated he balance his time and energy more effectively.

"There's a craziness to [Meyer], and I mean that in a good way," Long said. "Not only in sports, but in life. There has to be craziness in a coach to get something done. I see it in this guy."

Woody endured similar coaching rigors. Long said "he sacrificed family and everything for his job."

"He had a single-minded approach to everything, and that was football," said Larry Catuzzi, who coached under Woody from 1965 to 1967. "His life, other than his military career, was football. And he devoted all of his time, at some expense of his family, I thought, to football."

Meyer acknowledges some of the parallels. Despite first saying he had never thought about the comparison, he proceeded to list three of Woody's traits that he also values: love and care for the players, demanding a lot from the players, and placing a premium on academics.

Those are all virtues that Otis has noticed as well. The loyalty, compassion, obsession, and drive—all of those quirks that contributed to Woody's legacy at Ohio State—seem apparent in Meyer, too. They certainly have their wealth of differences. After all, Meyer lets his assistant coaches craft their own offensive and defensive schemes.

Still, where there is Urban, there is a bit of Woody, too.

"He's pretty tough, but he's fair and he's good to the kids," Otis said. "He will fight for them all the way, and that's how Woody was. When it comes down to nut-cracking time, they're going to fight for him.

"He's got some of that in him and he should."

. . . .

Urban Legend

For a long time, Urban Meyer refused to utter the word *lose*. The habit hit its stride when his Buckeyes rattled off 24 consecutive victories upon his arrival in Columbus.

"That 'L' word is not a good word for anyone," said Meyer, who added that he tries to avoid it at all costs.

Fortunately for him, he has not had to dabble much in the world of failure. In his first three seasons at Ohio State, Meyer compiled a 38–3 record. His team lost once at the Horseshoe, once at Lucas Oil Stadium in the Big Ten Championship, and once in south Florida at

Urban Meyer racked up a 38–3 record in his first three seasons as Ohio State's head coach.

the Orange Bowl. That is it. Three years, three measly defeats. Three years, only three encounters with disappointment.

In those three years, Meyer's teams conquered every conference foe during the regular season. Down to his third quarterback, he directed Ohio State to the College Football Playoff Championship in January 2015. A year earlier, he led his squad to within a few plays of a berth in the national title game. In his first year as Buckeyes head honcho, Meyer guided Ohio State to a 12–0 mark.

The first season might be the most remarkable, given that Meyer took over the reins of a team that had sputtered through a purgatorial 6–7 season mired in controversy, uncertainty, and discomfort. For the first time in nearly a quarter-century, the Buckeyes amassed a losing record. Luke Fickell had served as interim head coach in place of Jim Tressel, with whom the university parted ways following an exhaustive NCAA violations scandal. Quarterback Terrelle Pryor bolted early for the NFL, leaving overmatched veteran Joe Bauserman and unprepared freshman Braxton Miller to take the snaps. A few days after Thanksgiving, and two days after Ohio State dropped a 40–34 contest at Michigan, Meyer was announced as the university's new football coach.

Everyone knew that Meyer would be taking over a fractured program. Sure, the cracks in the armor could be healed, especially with a two-time national champion and an elite recruiter and motivator as its new head coach. But Meyer was a bit fractured, too. Meyer retired, then unretired, in 2009 because of health concerns. After the 2010 season, he left Florida for good, citing those same concerns, which included chest pains and other stress-related medical issues.

"It's something you have to drastically watch," Meyer said. "I sought counsel from guys I have great respect for. The bottom line is, it's just keeping things in order, as far as balance. There are only so many hours you can put into this job. Our staff, at times we've tried to overcome any issues we have by just spending more time in the office and more time at work."

That does not fly any longer. Upon taking the opening at Ohio State, Meyer was required by his family to sign a contract that promised his wife and three children that he would strike a more appropriate balance between his work and his family. Meyer said he has notes set up around his office to remind him to get out of the office at a fair hour "and go do the right thing."

"I'm trying. It's a daily battle with me," Meyer said. "I completely let it go at one point."

Striving for perfection took its toll on Meyer at Florida. Satisfaction was a foreign concept to the coach. Shades of that persona remain

JOIN THE RIVALRY

A brown-haired, mustache-wearing, 21-year-old graduate assistant at Ohio State named Urban Meyer made his commute to work one Monday morning in 1986. As he passed Lincoln and Morrill Towers, he noticed sheets hanging from the two massive dorm-filled pillars overlooking Ohio Stadium. The sheets displayed a message that was impossible to miss.

"Muck Fichigan"

At that moment, Meyer began to comprehend the magnitude of Ohio State's rivalry with Michigan.

"I said, 'That is really cool right there,'" Meyer said. "And they did, they switched the 'M' and the 'F,' and someone made them take it down. So that was in 1986, so there is some old student now that is laughing their tail off, saying, 'Yeah, that was my room.'"

in the man who now makes the final calls in Columbus. As Ohio State mounted a school record–long winning streak in 2013, Meyer continued to pinpoint flaws in the team's play. Even in 2012, when he morphed a 6–7 group into an undefeated bunch, he was less than thrilled.

"Early in the season our first year, I was very alarmed," Meyer said. "We weren't playing very hard. We weren't playing very smart. I had a brand new coaching staff that I was concerned about."

That foot rarely leaves the accelerator. Meyer points to his 2008 Florida team as one that proved elite in every single facet of the game. That year, the Gators knocked off Oklahoma in the BCS

Meyer was raised in Ashtabula, Ohio, a little less than 200 miles from Ohio State's campus, but he said he never really grasped the depth of the rivalry until he became a part of it.

"I didn't realize it, because I was just like most, that from the outside looking in, 'Hey, it's a really great game,'" Meyer said. "I grew up in the Ten Year War, and I learned to dislike Michigan at a very young age. But, no, you never really appreciate it until you're behind the walls here and find out how serious it is."

Meyer probably will never hang an obscene banner from the window of his Dublin, Ohio, home, but he quickly expended plenty of energy emphasizing the significance of the rivalry upon his arrival at Ohio State.

"Do we make a big deal out of this game? Absolutely," Meyer said. "Do we make a huge deal, over the top, about rivalry games? Yes, we do. That's the way I was brought up. We kind of go over the top here, and we always have. A new coach doesn't come in here and try to stimulate that rivalry. That rivalry has been stimulated a long time ago, and we need to carry it on and make it stronger."

Championship Game and walloped their opponents by an average of 31 points. In four regular-season affairs against ranked foes, they outscored the competition 201–52. And yet, Meyer never propped his feet up on the extension of his recliner, beer in hand, and reflected on the dominance he exacted from his players and the glory in which he reveled as the confetti sprayed across Sun Life Stadium in Miami. Not until he removed himself from his job and the sport for a year did he realize he never awarded himself time to relax, to reflect, to recharge. He was running himself into the ground. Quite literally, in fact.

His health scare preceded a stint at ESPN, where he served as a college football analyst until he accepted the position at Ohio State.

Three short years later, he had reached the pinnacle with his new school.

"What impresses me the most," said former Ohio State running back Eddie George, "is how he's been able to establish his culture, his thumbprint on the program and really redefine and transform what he wants them to be and along the way, he's winning ball games."

That unquenchable thirst for perfection still exists. Maybe Meyer is not as parched as he was when he coached under the powerful Florida sun, but he remains in search of the fountain of supremacy. On a gray mid-November afternoon in Champaign, Illinois, in 2013, Meyer stood at a podium on a small stage in an undersized interview room. Reporters lined the walls on both sides. Cameramen squeezed into a congested row in the back of the room. Never has a postgame press conference area been so cramped, so crowded, so uncomfortable, and so unaccommodating. And never did Meyer sound so vulnerable.

Ohio State had toppled Illinois 60–35 at Memorial Stadium, the Buckeyes' 28-point lead having dwindled to 12 midway through the fourth quarter. A pair of Carlos Hyde touchdowns in the closing minutes removed any doubt from the outcome of the game, but the Buckeyes attracted plenty of criticism for a lackluster performance—defensively, at least—in the resume-fueled race toward a BCS Championship Game berth.

Earlier in the week, Meyer had spoken with his team about the BCS rankings and where the Buckeyes stood in the mad dash to Pasadena, California. After watching his team struggle to deliver the knockout punch to the Fighting Illini, a team riding a 19-game conference losing streak, Meyer admitted some regret in focusing on the national landscape.

"I have to make sure our focus is on just getting better each week, instead of all the national stuff," Meyer said. "I am learning: Just shut your mouth and quit worrying about this and that. Let's get a little better."

That moment in that sardine can of a room offered the first taste of Meyer looking anything other than invincible in his two years at the helm with Ohio State. The Buckeyes had not lost since he had arrived in Columbus. He had maintained his patented style of handing out a limited amount of praise and keeping his players on their toes and avoiding any form of complacency. On this afternoon, though, he caved a bit. Sure, he had a bit of a flawed team, one with some visible deficiencies. Yet, given a relatively manageable schedule, a hard-nosed coach who was never content, and an abundance of talent at a few key positions, Ohio State remained in the national title picture until the first week of December.

Meyer ranted about style points and computer rankings, topics he did not have to worry about when the Buckeyes crept into the national title picture a year later, the first season judged by the College Football Playoff committee. He knew that with a porous secondary, an inconsistent passing attack, and a lack of depth at the linebacker position, his team need not worry about its placement on the national totem pole. If he was far from satisfied with his squad, how could the computers' algorithms be convinced of the Buckeyes' ability? Once Ohio State finished 12–2 in Meyer's second year, center Corey Linsley noted how such a record would earn other schools statues and banners, but in Columbus, it is just considered another ho-hum season with a BCS bowl game appearance. That standard is reflective of the benchmarks established at the university. It also reflects the barometer by which Meyer measures his teams and himself.

Meyer may have unearthed a better balance between work and family, but his endless quest for perfection followed him back to his home state. It did not take him long to climb to the top of the mountain at Ohio State. When Eli Apple intercepted Marcus Mariota's pass and the clock struck zero, Meyer captured his third national title in eight years. The idea of perfection went out the window in Week 2, when the Buckeyes fell short against Virginia Tech at home. They did not slip up again, though. Meyer bested his former SEC adversary, Nick Saban, and his Alabama Crimson Tide in the College Football Playoff semifinals. Ohio State sprinted past

Oregon en route to a three-touchdown victory in the title game. Just three seasons into his reign—and just two with bowl eligibility—Meyer delivered Columbus its first crystal football in more than a decade. More importantly, he never had much of a reason to say that dreaded "L" word.

. . . .

Trace the Lineage of Earle Bruce

Proud, confident, and beaming about the play of his receivers, Zach Smith returned home, where he encountered his two-year-old son, Cameron.

"Hey, did you watch the wideouts play? Did you watch Daddy's players play?" Smith asked his kid. "They played pretty well, huh?"

Without hesitation and with the disposition of a harsh critic, Cameron replied.

"No," he said. "Not Philly. He dropped that one pass."

Tough crowd.

Corey "Philly" Brown, the former captain of Ohio State's receiving corps, the group Smith advises as one of Urban Meyer's assistants, tallied six catches for 127 yards in that contest. Maybe Cameron Smith is preparing for the day he paces the sideline at Ohio Stadium. After all, coaching is in his blood. His father has done it at Florida, Marshall, Temple, and Ohio State. His great-grandfather is Earle Bruce.

Zach Smith did not map out passing routes on his Etch A Sketch. He did not ditch his pacifier for a whistle. He did not dig through his toy box in search of a clipboard. He did, from a young age, have dreams of surveying the green grass at the Horseshoe, watching his players put his tutelage to use. That vision stemmed from his adoration for Bruce, who served as the Buckeyes' head coach from 1979 to 1987.

"I was a four-year-old kid walking around with a superhero-like admiration for his grandfather and what he did," Smith said. "When you're a little kid, you can be anything when you grow up and there was no confusion in my life of what I wanted that to be."

By the time he attended Dublin Coffman High School, just outside of Columbus, Smith was certain.

"He talked about it when he started playing football," Bruce said. "He wanted to be a coach at Ohio State."

Smith remembers observing practice, watching "giants running around." He remembers the day Bruce received a pink slip and the Ohio State Marching Band showed up at the coach's house and performed the university's fight song. He remembers his summer trips to Colorado, where he would spend two and a half weeks with his grandparents, after Bruce took the head coaching gig at Colorado State. Smith remembers the bond he shared with his grandparents. He was especially close with his grandmother, Jean.

Above all, though, Smith remembers the virtues he learned from Bruce, not the playbook analysis and coaching techniques the 2002 College Football Hall of Fame inductee shared with his grandson.

"X's and O's are the most overrated thing in coaching," Smith said. "Coaching is more about philosophical approaches to life. That really shaped my personality and who I am more than anything."

Bruce worked under Woody Hayes at Ohio State before he advanced to the head coaching positions at the University of Tampa and Iowa State. He then returned to Columbus as head coach when Hayes was dismissed after the Gator Bowl at the end of the 1978 season. Bruce was named the Big Ten Coach of the Year in his first season as Ohio State's boss, when his team fashioned an 11–1 mark. In nine years as head coach of the Buckeyes, he logged an 81–26–1 record, including 57–17 in Big Ten play. Ohio State won five of its eight bowl games under his leadership and the team won no fewer than nine games in any season except for his last as head coach.

Meyer served on Bruce's staff at Ohio State in 1986 and '87, when he coached the tight ends and wide receivers. Smith worked for Meyer at Florida from 2005 to 2009. He will never forget the day Meyer hired him at Ohio State. When Bruce got wind that Meyer was pegged as the man to resurrect the program in 2011, he immediately called his grandson.

"You need to try to get on his staff," Bruce said.

"Well no shit," Smith replied, joking that he would script a letter to his former boss.

Meyer and Smith had maintained a dialogue after Smith departed Gainesville, Florida, to coach the receivers at Marshall and then at Temple. A few days before Christmas in 2011, Meyer called Bruce and revealed he would be offering Smith a spot on his staff. Smith's grandfather learned of his hiring before he did. Still, Smith happened to be with Bruce at the time of the conversation, so it did not take long for the grandson to find out. Bruce said Smith has excelled under Meyer.

"There is no doubt about that," Bruce said.

Once cradled as a little kid by the massive paws of linebacker Chris Spielman, Smith earned the chance to coach at the only school about which he ever fantasized.

"The biggest point I make to anyone—players, kids, whoever it is—is if you want to do something, do it, but you have to go get it," Smith said. "You would think—my grandfather was the head coach at Ohio

State, he had all of these assistant coaches who worked for him and are loyal to him and love him for what he did to help their career, but no one is going to just give me a job. You have to go earn it."

What about Cameron, the toughest toddler in college football? Will the Bruce-Smith family tree eventually bear another coaching branch?

Said Smith, with a laugh: "I don't want to play for him."

Visit Lauren's Garden in Houston, Texas

A few times each month, when Larry Catuzzi has board meetings downtown, he will traverse the brick path in Lauren's Garden. He will listen to the persistent splashing of the fountain and look at the 40 large stones, the 184 small rocks, and the 2,753 pebbles that soak up the gentle flow of the water as a thick mist hovers above Houston's Market Square Park.

He will step past the gray benches, the cluster of trees, and the bronze sculpture of his daughter. The figure has forever captured the face of a 38-year-old woman with a zest for action, for skydiving and roller blading and hiking and kayaking, for squeezing the most out of life.

Lauren Grandcolas was not supposed to travel on September 11, 2001. She was not supposed to be on Flight 93.

Catuzzi was aware of the commitment. He knew all about Woody Hayes and the head coach's personality.

"Hey, you better be prepared to spend all your nights here, away from your family," the other assistant coaches told him when he joined Hayes' staff at Ohio State in 1965.

"Woody sacrificed family and everything for his job," said Bill Long, who played quarterback for the Buckeyes from 1965 to 1968. "There is no question about that."

And there was no question that his disciples would demonstrate the same drive.

Catuzzi spent a year at Dayton and four years at Indiana before he toughed out three more under Woody. Then and only then was he "ready to go out and conquer the world," Catuzzi said. He landed the head coaching vacancy at Williams College. Three years into that job, however, he yearned for "a saner life," one with more time for his wife, Barbara, and their three young daughters. He feared he would evolve into the work-obsessed creature in the short-sleeve white button-down and tie that roamed the Ohio State sideline for 28 years.

"You miss your family and you miss some of the things they did growing up," said Earle Bruce, an assistant coach at Ohio State who eventually took over for Hayes. "You didn't get to do anything during the football season except football."

So, Catuzzi left coaching and never looked back. He transitioned into the financial world and struck the balance between his career and his family for which he had longed. Each autumn, Larry and Barbara pack up their summer house at a Lake Toxaway resort in the Smoky Mountains of North Carolina and head back home to Houston. A few years ago, they planted some chestnut trees in Lauren's name.

Lauren was three months pregnant with her first child on 9/11. Would it have been a son with Lauren's bright blue eyes? A daughter who could not resist the temptation to explore the outdoors, just like her mother? Catuzzi will never know, but he knows this: Lauren would have treasured her family the way he did when he opted for a life in town, preparing financial analyses, instead of devising game plans on a chalkboard in a dark office.

Her family was the reason she switched her flight that day, after all. Lauren was traveling home to her husband in San Francisco, and she just wanted to get there faster.

At first, Catuzzi's voice quivers. Then he clears his throat and begins, forming the well-practiced words in a stoic manner sculpted into a monotone by the 12 years that have elapsed.

A day after the Catuzzi clan dispersed from New Jersey, where they had assembled for the funeral of Larry's mother, Larry and Barbara were in the car. One of their daughters called and asked them to pull off to the side of the road. She told them that Lauren's flight had been hijacked, and Larry jammed the gas pedal with everything he had, peeling off the shoulder into the haze of a nightmare.

Was Lauren on that plane? And if she was, why was she? Did she reschedule her flight? Could she have changed her mind without telling anyone? Could the passengers thwart the hijacking? Were they aware of the other planes that had been commandeered by terrorists? Could this all just be a misunderstanding?

Larry and Barbara arrived at their home to two voicemails: one from their minister and one from United Airlines. Flight 93 had crashed. Lauren was gone.

Shortly before Flight 93 plunged near Shanksville, Pennsylvania, Lauren left a voicemail for her husband, Jack Grandcolas. She said there was "a little problem" with the aircraft and she was "fine and comfortable." Maybe she was at peace with how much she had accomplished, like playing tennis and mountain biking and jogging and having served on the drill team at the University of Texas. Or, for having written the table of contents and the first chapter of *You Can Do It! The Merit Badge Handbook for Grown-Up Girls*, a book completed by her sisters, Dara and Vaughn, that encourages women to explore everything from cooking to rock climbing to financial planning.

"She just had a great lust for life," Catuzzi said. "Her motor ran 150 mph all the time."

And it is still running, through her parents. They established the Lauren Catuzzi Grandcolas Foundation, which raises money for women, children's health, and education and has helped fund hospitals, Girl Scouts groups, and college scholarships. Catuzzi has served on the Flight 93 Federal Advisory Commission, which orchestrated the construction of the Flight 93 Memorial in Shanksville.

"She was not a boastful girl," Catuzzi said. "She was a very modest girl. She would not look for this recognition at all, but it has helped us grieve and keep Lauren in our minds and memory."

As coaches, Catuzzi and Hayes had little in common. Long described the two as "night and day." Hayes flashed his emotion and temper during the most elementary activities, such as writing on the chalkboard in the locker room. Catuzzi remained much more composed and precise.

"Even when there was something very big or exciting that happened," Long said, "you'd get off the field and Coach Catuzzi was happy, but was always thinking about the next level, the next thing we'd do."

His career changed, but Catuzzi discovered ways to remain involved in football. In the 1980s, he became president of the sponsor of the Bluebonnet Bowl. He also served as the vice chairman of the Houston Sports Authority and is on the board of directors for the Texas Bowl.

"I'm a person who doesn't break away from things easily," Catuzzi said.

So, he and his wife worked with the city of Houston to build Lauren's Garden. The stones that rest on the fountain represent the victims of the attacks of that day. The city block is filled with flowers and trees and with solemn and uplifting reminders, such as the bristlecone pine, the bronze vine, and the granite medallion, which symbolize endurance and resilience.

Yes, Catuzzi could coach. He could command the respect of a feared icon in Hayes and he could recruit.

"He got some of the greatest players here," Bruce said.

Above all, though, Catuzzi valued family.

He knew it when he shook Hayes' hand on his first day at Ohio State, and he knows it when he walks through Lauren's Garden, past the food kiosk, the dog park, the flowers, the trees, and the granite walls, on his way to the bronze sculpture of his daughter.

"What we did in return is just one way that we could honor our daughter and honor the other victims of Flight 93 and 9/11," Catuzzi said. "Without that, we would have had a tremendous void in our lives. I always marveled at people who lost a child. How do you go on with life? But you do find a way."

. . . .

The Vest

When universities or professional teams hire a coach, the new boss often gushes about how he had dreamed of attaining his new gig since childhood. Jim Tressel had never considered the Division I college ranks, let alone Ohio State. Instead, he aspired to follow in the footsteps of his father, Lee Tressel, who racked up 155 victories while coaching for 23 seasons at Division III Baldwin-Wallace College in Berea, Ohio.

Tressel originally wanted to be a high school head coach. Instead, he became the head honcho at Youngstown State, where he compiled a 135–57–2 record in 15 years. He directed the Penguins to four Division I-AA National Championships.

Jim Tressel guided Ohio State to a national championship in his second season at the helm in 2002.

"I was convinced that I wanted to be there forever," Tressel said.

Then, Ohio State severed ties with coach John Cooper. They replaced him with Tressel, and suddenly, the man who grew up two hours north was tasked with upholding the tradition and responsibility of college football in Columbus.

"That's daunting," Tressel said.

The night he was hired, Tressel gave a speech at halftime of the Ohio State men's basketball game. In his monologue, he guaranteed that the football team would be prepared for nemesis Michigan 310 days later. Immediately, he prioritized that rivalry above all else. Tressel's teams proceeded to log a 9–1 record against their Big Ten foe.

"He followed through with that," said Ohio State football historian Jack Park.

Cooper was fired following a loss to South Carolina in the 2001 Outback Bowl, which capped an 8–4 season. In Tressel's first year at the helm, the Buckeyes compiled a 7–5 mark and another Outback Bowl loss to the Gamecocks. It was not exactly an ideal start to his term. Tressel suspended senior quarterback Steve Bellisari for the final two games following his arrest for drunk driving.

"There were ups and downs that year," Tressel said.

Tressel considered his first year a transition year. He built relationships with players, staff members, families, and high school coaches. He worked to change the culture of the program and lay the foundation for a bright future. He contended that he reached the goals he had established for his first year. And once the transition period ended, it was full steam ahead. The Buckeyes doubled their win total in Tressel's second year, becoming the first team in college football history to attain a 14–0 record. Ohio State capped its perfect season with an unforgettable 31–24 double-overtime victory against a heavily favored Miami Hurricanes team that entered the title game riding a nation-long 34-game winning streak.

EXTRA POINTS

Coaching Tree

The Buckeyes have had 24 coaches since they began play in 1890, though only six since Woody Hayes assumed the position in 1951. Here is a list of the program's coaches and their accomplishments.

1890: Alexander Lilley (3–5 record)

1892: Jack Ryder (19–17–1)

1896: Charles Hickey (5–5–1)

1897: David Edwards (1–7–1)

1898: Jack Ryder (3–5)

1899: John Eckstorm (22–4–3)

1902: Perry Hale (14–5–2)

1904: Edwin Sweetland (14–7–2)

1906: Albert Herrnstein (28–10–1)

1910: Howard Jones (6–1–3)

1911: Harry Vaughan (5–3–2)

1912: John Richards (6–3)

1913: John Wilce (78–33–9)

Tressel cited two reasons for Ohio State's swift ascent: the growth in relationships established during his first year in Columbus, and the hunger of the upperclassmen who had endured a couple of underwhelming seasons.

"They were not going to leave here without having an Ohio State–type season," Tressel said. "And then, the ball bounced right a couple of times and our guys kept fighting and it ended up being a good deal."

Tressel never again reached the pinnacle of college football while at Ohio State. The Buckeyes played in consecutive national title games

1929: Sam Willaman (26–10–5)

1934: Francis Schmidt (39–16–1)

1941: Paul Brown (18–8–1)

1944: Carroll Widdoes (16–2)

1946: Paul Bixler (4–3–2)

1947: Wes Fesler (21–13–3)

1951: Woody Hayes (205–61–10)

1979: Earle Bruce (81–26–1)

1988: John Cooper (111–43–4)

2001: Jim Tressel (94–21)

2011: Luke Fickell (6–7)

2012: Urban Meyer (38–3)

Hayes was responsible for five of the program's eight national championships. Widdoes (1944), Hayes (1957), Bruce (1979), and Tressel (2002) all earned the distinction of being the American Football Coaches Association Coach of the Year. Aside from Richards, who racked up a 5–0 mark in conference play in 1912, and Meyer, who owns a 24–0 record against Big Ten competition, Tressel boasts the best winning percentage in league play, with an .808 mark (59 wins and 14 losses). Hayes amassed a 152–37–7 record against Big Ten foes, good for a .793 winning percentage. The Buckeyes won 13 conference titles under his reign.

a few years later, but they fell short against Florida and LSU. Above another crystal football for his trophy case, though, the man in the sweater vest valued his time dedicated toward turning teenage boys into professional adults.

"I've got a whole box sitting right across from me on the counter of about 15 rings," Tressel said. "But you know what? Those rings, the dust is on them; they're just memories. But the progress a person makes, even if they stumble and fall—we stumble and fall individually and as a group—what's important is at the end of the day, they are ready to go out in this competitive world and see if they can battle their way through this tough, tough world."

Tressel stumbled.

He roamed the Ohio State sideline for 10 years with his conservative attire and conservative play-calling. He basked in the glory of a national championship and took heat for twice falling just short in the quest to capture another crystal football. And after a decade of leadership and one tumultuous offseason shrouded with controversy and scandal, Tressel was gone, forced to submit a letter of resignation on Memorial Day in 2011.

Tressel faced a five-game suspension—increased from an original two-game ban—and a $250,000 fine for failing to report NCAA violations committed by a handful of his players. In his letter, Tressel wrote that the turmoil within the football program had become too much of a distraction. Athletic director Gene Smith said the university planned to retain Tressel until the backing for such a measure eroded and external pressure heightened.

"The support had deteriorated for Jim," Smith said. "The brand of the institution was now at stake in a greater form. We were constantly under attack, and so when I sat down with him that Sunday night and had that conversation, there was no hesitation on his part when I asked him for his resignation."

Five months earlier, the NCAA suspended five players for five games for selling memorabilia and receiving improper benefits from the owner of a local tattoo parlor. Reports uncovered that Tressel had been aware of the situation for more than six months, despite the fact that the coach signed a document on September 13, 2010, stating that he had no knowledge of any NCAA violations. Six months later, he admitted to knowingly playing athletes who should have been deemed ineligible. At that point, Tressel believed he should keep his job, saying, "That wouldn't be something that would jump in my mind, unless there came that point in time where I said, 'You know what? The best thing to do for those kids is if I do.'"

That point in time arrived a little more than two months later.

"You can't babysit every single player on your team," said linebacker James Laurinaitis. "If a kid gets a DUI, are you going to blame the kid or blame the parents?"

Malcolm Jenkins, who played cornerback under Tressel from 2005 to 2008, said Tressel always looked out for his players' best interests.

"He didn't automatically go snitch on his five players," Jenkins said. "He withheld it, which is wrong by NCAA standards, but he's looking out for these kids like they're his own. He could have been selfish and saved his neck."

Tressel was careful, deliberate, and almost timid. His approach earned him the nickname "The Senator." Some questioned how those attributes played out on the field, but few questioned the success he achieved despite them. Off the field, it helped him cultivate an image of perfection. That ultimately set him up to fail.

"[Everyone] thought he was perfect," Laurinaitis said. "That's the kind of thing that bothers me. Everyone makes mistakes and he'd be the first to admit it."

Whether the ending overshadows his 9–1 mark against Michigan, his national title team, his seven Big Ten crowns—that is up to the eye of the beholder. Tressel was not the first Ohio State coach whose tenure ended on less-than-ideal terms and he accomplished plenty during his time on the sideline at the Horseshoe. He was inducted into the Ohio State Athletics Hall of Fame in Fall 2015.

"His legacy here as far as football at Ohio State will always be extremely high," Park said. "It's been tarnished a little bit at the end because of his resignation. The same thing happened to Woody Hayes."

At the end of each football game at Ohio Stadium, fans join the team in a rendition of "Carmen Ohio."

Sing "Carmen Ohio" with the Team

After every Ohio State football game, the players and coaches, arms wrapped around each other, gather near the university's marching band for a rendition of "Carmen Ohio." After home affairs at Ohio Stadium, the team will stand in the southeast corner of the end zone, peering up toward the band and the student section. They join in harmony for the first verse of the tune, the oldest still woven into the school's fabric today.

Oh come, let's sing Ohio's praise

And songs to Alma Mater raise

While our hearts, rebounding, thrill

With joy which death alone can still

Summer's heat or winter's cold

The seasons pass, the years will roll

Time and change will surely show

How firm thy friendship, O-hi-o

THE VOICE

Cie Grant rushed in from the blind side, harassed Miami quarterback Ken Dorsey, and forced an incompletion. The Buckeyes poured out onto the field from the sideline and celebrated a national championship. Two weeks later, at a snow-covered Ohio Stadium on a 20-degree afternoon on January 18, 2003, Ohio State celebrated again.

The Ohio State Marching Band completed its Script Ohio tradition on the field. Players, draped in red parkas, spoke to the crowd. Grant then led the seniors in a rendition of "Carmen Ohio." Grant put on display a silky, smooth singing voice as he voiced the words of the alma mater into the microphone. When he finished the first verse, his teammates playfully shook him to congratulate him on an impressive performance. The band then played another verse.

Grant instantly became synonymous with the school's song. His delivery became implemented into Ohio State football lore. It served as a means of inspiration for fans and players in subsequent seasons. Prior to the Buckeyes' national championship clash with Oregon on January 12, 2015, Grant recorded a message for the team, via the Ohio State athletic department, in which he wished his alma mater luck and then performed the first verse of "Carmen, Ohio." He could not resist breaking out into a big smile after he voiced the "O-hi-o" at the end of a verse, as he added, "Go Bucks."

The origin of "Carmen Ohio" is debated, though the creator of the song is undisputed. Fred Cornell, an athlete, amateur poet, and member of Ohio State's glee club, penned the lyrics during his student years near the beginning of the 20th century. There are two tales used to explain the composition of the tune. One contends that on a miserable train ride back from Ann Arbor, Michigan, in 1902 after the rival Wolverines pounded the Buckeyes 86–0 in football, Cornell scripted the song. The other story suggests that Cornell adhered to a request from the men's glee club in 1903 to write the song.

These jolly days of priceless worth

By far the gladdest days on earth

Soon will pass and we not know

How dearly we love O-hi-o

We should strive to keep thy name

Of fair repute and spotless fame

So in college halls we'll grow

And love thee better, O-hi-o

No matter the story preferred, both tales recount that the song was performed publicly for the first time by the glee club in 1903. The song and its moniker have become institutional in university lore. The school's website for students to submit documents or find class notes is called "Carmen."

Though age may dim our memory's store

We'll think of happy days of yore

True to friend and frank to foe

As sturdy sons of O-hi-o

If on seas of care we roll

'Neath blackened sky or barren shoal

Thoughts of thee bid darkness go

Dear alma mater, O-hi-o

Chapter 2

Notable Players

Celebrate Archie Griffin Day

The most awkward moment of the 2013 Big Ten Championship Game came after Michigan State pulled away with a 34–24 victory against Ohio State. Archie Griffin, the former Ohio State running back, had to present Spartans quarterback Connor Cook with the Griffin-Grange Championship Game Most Valuable Player Trophy. Two months earlier, Griffin had predicted that if the Buckeyes remained undefeated through the conference title game, Urban Meyer's group would sneak into the BCS Championship Game. Ohio State followed his plan for a while, only to come up short in the final leg of the season-long race. And in the end, Griffin, perhaps the face of Ohio State football throughout the years, had to hand some hardware to the player who just picked apart his alma mater's defense.

Such is life for the running back so nice he won the Heisman Trophy twice. He is the only player in college football history to accomplish that feat. In Griffin's four years at Ohio State, the Woody Hayes–led Buckeyes lost a grand total of five games.

Griffin originally wanted to attend Northwestern, though. Rudy Hubbard, a running back at Ohio State from 1965 to 1967 and an assistant coach thereafter, helped court him to Columbus. While a physical education major at Ohio State, Hubbard was a student-teacher with Bob Stewart, Griffin's high school coach at Eastmoor High School. Hubbard and Stewart always talked football. Stewart was a bit disgruntled with Ohio State for not giving his high school program the sort of attention he thought it deserved. Thus, he reallocated his loyalty to Indiana's program.

Archie Griffin won a pair of Heisman Trophies while at Ohio State, the only player in college football history to accomplish such a feat.

When Griffin ascended through the high school ranks, Hubbard was an assistant coach and had a hand in recruiting. Hubbard planned to use his relationship with Stewart to lure Griffin to Ohio State.

"I think that opened the doors," Hubbard said.

By the time Hubbard had a chance to speak with Griffin for the first time, the sought-after tailback had already visited Northwestern. Griffin seemed poised to venture off to Evanston, Illinois. Hubbard got the inclination that the high schooler did not want to join a college football factory. Academics were an important factor in his decision as well.

Griffin eventually made his way to Ohio State's campus, and he settled on the university, where he would end up spending four magical years. Hubbard coached the running backs—though Woody claimed to preside over that position group—and had been campaigning for playing time for the freshman. Griffin's first year at Ohio State in 1972 marked the first year that freshmen were eligible to play.

The Buckeyes had toppled Iowa 21–0 in the season opener in Columbus. They had a bye week the following week before a September 30 matchup against North Carolina at the Horseshoe. Woody and the coaching staff took the first-, second-, and third-string players to a hotel the night before a game to keep them away from any potential distractions on campus and to ensure a full night of rest. Those on the fourth and fifth strings would remain in the dorm rooms and simply meet the team at the stadium the next day to go through the pregame walkthrough. Griffin was listed as the fifth-string tailback at the time, so he stayed in his dorm room, even though Hubbard had been singing the freshman's praises to Woody all week.

QUICK FACTS

- Only five players in team history have registered multiple 200-yard rushing games: Eddie George (five), Archie Griffin, Beanie Wells, Carlos Hyde, and Ezekiel Elliott.

- Pete Johnson (1973–76) holds the program record with 56 career rushing touchdowns. Keith Byars ranks second with 46, followed by Eddie George with 44.

- Eddie George logged the most 100-yard games in a season in school history with 12 in 1995. Archie Griffin twice tallied 11 such games in one year (1973, 1974) and 10 such games once (1975). Carlos Hyde (2013) and Ezekiel Elliott (2014) accomplished the feat nine times in a single season.

"I know Griffin is our fifth-team tailback," Hubbard told Woody, "but he's had such an excellent week of practice. I think you ought to give this kid a shot."

Woody ultimately listened to Hubbard and sprung the 18-year-old into action. Late in the first quarter, Griffin was summoned. He was so surprised by the call that he jogged about halfway out to the huddle before he realized he was missing his helmet. He strapped on the equipment and proceeded to tally an Ohio State single-game record 239 yards on the ground in Ohio State's 29–14 victory against the Tar Heels.

The next day, the *Columbus Dispatch* included a line about Griffin in which the paper's sports editor said that never before in the 50-year history of Ohio Stadium had one player ever pleased the crowd with such outstanding play.

"After one game, he became a real star," said Ohio State football historian Jack Park.

Griffin eclipsed his own record the following year, when he rushed for 246 yards in a win against Iowa. He rattled off an NCAA record stretch of 31 consecutive contests with at least 100 rushing yards. In all, he totaled 34 games in his college career with at least 100 yards on the ground. He rushed for 867 yards as a freshman, 1,577 yards as a sophomore, 1,695 yards as a junior, and 1,450 yards as a senior. He won the Heisman Trophy after his junior and senior seasons. Ohio State amassed a 40–5–1 record during his tenure in Columbus, and the Buckeyes claimed the Big Ten title and advanced to the Rose Bowl in each of his four seasons. He twice earned the *Chicago Tribune*'s Silver Football, given to the Big Ten Most Valuable Player. Woody once called Griffin "the best football player I've ever seen." The old coach frequently lauded the running back's personal traits as well.

Griffin was elected to Ohio State's "Varsity O" Hall of Fame in 1981 and to the College Football Hall of Fame in 1986. He was inducted into the Rose Bowl Hall of Fame in 1990, and on January 1, 2014, he was named the All-Century Player of the Rose Bowl during the celebration of the 100th edition of the contest. In 1996, he was enshrined in his high school's hall of fame and Eastmoor Academy renamed its playing field "Archie Griffin Field." The Buckeyes football program retired his No. 45 in 1999.

On July 17, 2013, Ohio governor John Kasich wrote and passed a resolution that declared that 45 days prior to each season's opening kickoff would be considered "Archie Griffin Day." The resolution read:

"Whereas, in 1972, a young Ohio man by the name of Archie Griffin arrived at The Ohio State University ready to play football and make Buckeyes history; and whereas, while setting numerous school, conference, and NCAA records, he remained a shining example of humility and compassion on and off the field; and whereas, in fact, the legendary coach Woody Hayes once described Griffin by

EXTRA POINTS

A Different Era

Archie Griffin played in an era in which running games and defense reigned supreme on Saturday afternoons. Woody Hayes would have laughed at the thought of a spread offense, with a mobile quarterback and backs and receivers in the slot who could run four-second 40-yard dashes with their eyes closed.

Griffin excelled in Hayes' system, as he recorded perhaps the greatest career of any tailback in Ohio State football history. Still, he is confident in how he would have fared in Urban Meyer's power spread offense.

"I think I would have fared very well," Griffin said. "The fact of the matter is, in this offense, you get a chance to get out in space. When I played, we were off-tackle a lot and you were running boxed in with the box stacked against you, the whole works, and I was still able to have some success. That was mainly due to the great linemen we had playing for us at Ohio State.

"A back's dream is to get out in space and try to make people miss and see what kind of yards they can gain in those situations."

saying, 'he's a better young man than he is a football player, and he's the best football player I've ever seen;' and whereas, to this day Griffin remains the only student-athlete to earn college football's most prestigious award, the Heisman Trophy, on two separate occasions; and whereas, as one of Ohio's greatest role models and leaders, Griffin has been a symbol of hard work and determination throughout his great state; and whereas, since Griffin's reign on the gridiron, he has remained active and loyal to his Buckeye roots and is currently serving as the president and CEO of the Ohio State Alumni Association—a network of nearly 500,000 alumni; and whereas, he wore the number 45 on his jersey throughout his tremendous collegiate career, and it is only fitting that today, 45 days from the Buckeyes' football season opener, be named in his honor. Now,

RUNNING IN PLACE

Archie Griffin holds the illustrious title of being the only player in college football to claim two Heisman Trophy awards, but he does not hold the single-season rushing record at his own school. Here is a list of Ohio State rushing records.

Most rushing yards in a single season:

1. Eddie George: 1,927 (1995, 12 games)

2. Ezekiel Elliott: 1,878 (2014, 15 games)

3. Keith Byars: 1,764 (1984, 12 games)

4. Archie Griffin: 1,695 (1974, 12 games)

5. Beanie Wells: 1,609 (2007, 13 games)

6. Archie Griffin: 1,577 (1973, 11 games)

7. Tim Spencer: 1,538 (1982, 12 games)

8. Carlos Hyde: 1,521 (2013, 11 games)

9. Pepe Pearson: 1,484 (1996, 12 games)

10. Archie Griffin: 1,450 (1975, 12 games)

Most rushing yards in a single game:

1. Eddie George: 314 (1995, 36 carries)

2. Keith Byars: 274 (1984, 39 carries)

3.   (tie) Archie Griffin: 246 (1973, 30 carries)

Ezekiel Elliott: 246 (2014, 36 carries)

Carlos Hyde: 246 (2013, 24 carries)

6.   Archie Griffin: 239 (1972, 27 carries)

7.   Raymont Harris: 235 (1993, 39 carries)

8.   (tie) Ezekiel Elliott: 230 (2014, 20 carries)

Maurice Clarett: 230 (2002, 31 carries)

10.   Ollie Cline: 229 (1945, 32 carries)

Most rushing yards in a career:
1.   Archie Griffin: 5,589 (1972–75)

2.   Eddie George: 3,768 (1992–95)

3.   Tim Spencer: 3,553 (1979–82)

4.   Beanie Wells: 3,382 (2006–08)

5.   Keith Byars: 3,200 (1982–85)

6.   Carlos Hyde: 3,198 (2010–13)

7.   Pepe Pearson: 3,076 (1994–97)

8.   Braxton Miller: 3,054 (2011–13)

9.   Carlos Snow: 2,999 (1987–90, 1991)

10.   Michael Wiley: 2,951 (1996–99)

therefore, I, John R. Kasich, Governor of the State of Ohio, do hereby recognize July 17, 2013 as Archie Griffin Day throughout Ohio and encourage all citizens to take part in the observance of this day and to take note of the positive impact Archie Griffin has had on our communities."

Griffin left behind quite a legacy at Ohio State. His son spent three seasons with the Buckeyes as well. Adam Griffin, a 5'8" defensive back, was part of the school's 2010 recruiting class. As a third-year sophomore in 2012, he played in all 12 games on special teams. Shoulder surgery ended his career in the fall of 2013.

Of course, Griffin is most remembered for the award he merited twice during his four years on campus: the Heisman Trophy. Andre Ware, the recipient of the hardware in 1989, called Griffin "the godfather of the group" and "the standard." Ohio State coach Urban Meyer referred to him as a role model and "the ultimate." Griffin has always maintained his modesty. He will not mind if another player one day joins him in the exclusive pantheon of two-time Heisman Trophy winners.

"I would absolutely welcome another guy winning it twice," Griffin said. "I've been one who has said for the longest that there will be another two-time Heisman Trophy winner and now I believe there could even be a three-time Heisman Trophy winner when you see that they're giving the awards to freshmen or redshirt freshmen. So I think there's a possibility that there could be a three-time Heisman Trophy winner, but I think there will definitely be a two-time Heisman Trophy winner."

Grab a Bite at Eddie George's Grille 27

WHERE: 1636 N. High Street, Columbus, Ohio, 43201

WHEN: 11:00 AM to 12:00 AM Sunday to Wednesday, 11:00 AM to 2:00 AM Thursday to Saturday

HOW TO DO IT: Sit at a table and be waited on or sit at the bar, a setup with plenty of TVs, beers on tap, and Ohio State memorabilia

COST FACTOR: Burgers are $9-12, appetizers are $6-12, entrees range from $12-20

BUCKET RANK: 🪣 🪣

· ·

All eyes were on Eddie George, his jersey tucked tightly around his midsection, the ball in his possession, while the tailback was at Ohio State. He established the school record for rushing yards in a season in 1995 when he totaled 1,927 yards on the ground. That season, he captured the Heisman Trophy and a slew of other awards. He proceeded to the NFL as a first-round draft selection of the Houston Oilers. Later, Ohio State retired his No. 27 jersey, and in 2011, he was elected into the College Football Hall of Fame.

After his playing days expired, George diversified his interests. He became a familiar face as a football analyst. He earned his master's in business from Northwestern University. He made cameo appearances on a number of TV shows. He also opened up a pair of restaurants, including one in his old stomping grounds.

Consider High Street the line of scrimmage for Eddie George's Grille 27 on Ohio State's campus. It resides at the corner of the main road and Chittenden Ave., within walking distance for students both on and off campus.

The restaurant is owned by the G.R.E.A.T. Grille Group, which has also opened spots for former running back Jerome Bettis, the Indianapolis Colts, and the Houston Texans.

George's domain towers over passersby, with a giant glass window protecting a tall, white wall with a red-painted number 27. The glass sits atop a rotunda, above which the name of the restaurant is perched. The location has a moderate-sized patio in front of the building. Inside, a bar area—rife with TVs—awaits to the right and a common dining setup sits to the left. The restaurant claims nearly 60 flat-screen, high-definition TVs that constantly feed live sports action to its customers. Audio from the sports game or show of the moment is pumped through speakers both inside and outside the restaurant. Those strolling down High Street can hear the action.

The restaurant also boasts a private party room that can host up to 150 people. It contains a private bar and, of course, more high-definition TVs.

The menu consists of typical pub fare—wings, nachos, sliders—as well as salads, burgers, sandwiches, and a handful of steaks and seafood dishes. A short list of chef's signatures includes mac and cheese (with a crispy bread crumb crust, bacon, and tomato), fried chicken (with an herb cream sauce), the Burger 27 (a blend of short rib and chuck, infused with bacon), a twice-grilled barbecue burrito (with grilled chicken, sautéed peppers and onions, cheese, and barbecue sauce), and "the garbage plate," which includes a mac and cheese cake, a sloppy joe, an over easy egg, and sweet rooster sauce.

Clearly, "the garbage plate" is not something George consumed during his college days, when he made a habit out of dashing toward the end zone, all while his jersey was rolled up to show off his figure.

Special Teams

There are those August afternoons in Columbus, the ones with the potent heat and oppressive humidity, the ones that sap the spirit from a football player forced to run sprints and do push-ups. As he bends his elbows and the tip of his nose touches the grass, sweat drips off of his face and falls to the ground.

Those days conjure up memories for Craig Cataline. Really, those days are not all that bad. There were days in which Cataline stood guard on an oil platform in the Persian Gulf, days in which a sinister Mother Nature pushed the temperature toward 120 degrees, with the humidity approaching 100 percent and a torturous wind blowing in from the south like a space heater on full blast.

"You'd just be sweating all day," Cataline said. "You just have to drink water. There's nothing you can do."

The lack of a watch on his wrist often made time seem to stand still out there. Eventually, though, the clock struck midnight on his four-year stint in the navy, and in the years following, Cataline made his mark on Ohio State's special teams unit, so much so that Urban Meyer listed him as one of his favorite players on the 2013 team.

"He's just so damn tough," Meyer said. "He's tough as nails. He goes as hard as he possibly can and there's no doubt he's all in."

Cataline's two older brothers, Ryan and Eric, both served in the army and spent time overseas in Iraq and Kuwait. Cataline followed suit, thinking that it would ultimately function as a way to pay for college tuition. So, he enlisted in the military and trained in Pensacola, Florida, before working as an aircraft mechanic on an Air Force base in Omaha, Nebraska. After two years, he volunteered to venture overseas.

ARMED FORCES

Jim Tressel always had an affinity for the armed forces. He constantly praised Navy and what the program stood for in the week leading up to Ohio State's season opener in 2009.

"At Ohio State," Tressel said, "you can't win enough games and you can't visit enough patients in the hospital and you can't write enough encouraging notes to the military and you can't send out enough little football cards to the kids that write in."

Before the game, Ohio State displayed its respect for the Naval Academy with a video tribute and several honorary awards. The teams broke customary tradition by entering the field at the same time and running down the field together.

Navy did not just show up at Ohio Stadium for a feel-good story, though. The Midshipmen nearly delivered the Buckeyes a season-altering blow before the calendar flipped to September. After the pregame presentation and flyover prior to kickoff, Navy gave Ohio State all it could handle. In fact, a two-point conversion separated the Midshipmen and Buckeyes with two minutes remaining, but it was Ohio

"I remember my brother saying, 'It's like an adventure, so just go with the flow,'" Cataline said. "'It'll be over eventually.'"

Cataline was stationed in Kuwait, where he adhered to a regimented routine. Each shift, the troops woke up, ate breakfast, gathered weapons, dispersed into an assembly of Suburbans, and drove 20 minutes to a large industrial fort. The soldiers patrolled the area surrounding the main gate, referred to as an "entry control point," as cargo was shipped in and out of the port. The platform pumped out

State that came away with those coveted points en route to a nerve-racking 31–27 victory before more than 105,000 fans at the Horseshoe.

"They're the best in the world at what they do," said quarterback Terrelle Pryor. "They never give up. They're fighters."

With Ohio State gripping a 29–27 lead late in the fourth quarter, linebacker Brian Rolle intercepted a pass from Navy quarterback Ricky Dobbs on a two-point conversion attempt. Rolle returned it the length of the field for two points, as the stunned crowd released a collective sigh of relief. A Navy conversion would have tied the game, an almost unthinkable turn of events after the Midshipmen trailed by 15 midway through the fourth quarter.

"We were nervous for maybe a second," Rolle said.

On a wall in the Woody Hayes Athletic Center, where the football team practices and studies film, the team has a display honoring all Buckeyes who have served in the military. Each player has a black and red Block "O" bearing his name. The players are split into the five branches of the service: Air Force, Navy, Army, Marine Corps, and Coast Guard. Legendary Ohio State head coach Woody Hayes served in the U.S. Navy during World War II. Ohio State football historian Jack Park said Woody considered serving his country "one of the highlights of his life."

loads of drilled oil, which was funneled onto big tankers that Cataline and his cohorts marshaled in.

All in all, Cataline was not dashing through the thick, sweltering heat to avoid gunfire, but he did keep busy and carry out necessary tasks.

"It wasn't like anyone was storming the beach at Normandy," Cataline said. "There weren't huge battles. There was a lot to do out there, a lot of missions. It was pretty cool."

An Ohio State fan poses with members of the United States Naval Academy before the Buckeyes' game against Navy in 2009.

Following four years in the navy, Cataline attended Embry-Riddle Aeronautical University in Prescott, Arizona. After one semester, the native of Grandview Heights, Ohio, returned home. It was time to complete his dream.

"I had planned on walking on at Ohio State the whole time," Cataline said, "I just didn't know exactly how I was going to do it. All along, it's what I wanted to do."

Two games into his first season of action at Ohio State, Cataline absorbed a knee to his thigh, which then swelled up so much that it cut off circulation to his leg. He missed the remainder of the season. In 2013, he became a mainstay on Ohio State's kickoff coverage.

Meyer referred to him as "very powerful" and "a very valuable guy on our team." He raved about Cataline's leadership ability, noting that though his teammates were sometimes "intimidated" by him, "they love and respect him."

Cataline did not want his military background to serve as justification for commanding adoration.

"I'd rather it be because I make plays," he said.

He did. Against Penn State on October 26, 2013, Cataline earned the distinction of a "champion," an honor doled out to players who grade out at the highest levels during games.

"He's probably the best I've ever seen," said receiver Corey "Philly" Brown. "Nobody wants to block him. He's a big dude...so he just runs down and it doesn't matter what's there, he's just going to run through it, and that's what he does to people."

Cataline longed for those college days. He said he had to step back and gain perspective to realize where he was and where he has been.

"I grew up a Buckeyes fan my whole life," he said. "It's kind of amazing to be a part of this thing."

. . . .

Attend the Spring Game

On April 25, 2009, 95,722 people showed up at Ohio Stadium for a beach party. There was no sand, no water, and there were no seashells, but the university's football venue hosted nearly a full house of students, alumni, and more donning Hawaiian shirts, leis, shorts, sandals, and sunglasses.

With the temperature for the Saturday afternoon projected to hover around 80 degrees, early in the week the athletic department declared the 2009 spring game a Buckeye Beach Party. As the Ohio State football team held its annual scrimmage, fans kept one eye on the action and another on the inflatable beach balls being bounced around the stadium. Even head coach Jim Tressel sported a Hawaiian shirt in place of his patented sweater vest.

Ohio State's spring game dates back to at least the 1920s or '30s, though exact information is unclear and difficult to pinpoint. The athletic department owns evidence of the event only since 1988. The crowd of 95,722 in 2009 was the largest to attend a spring game—until 2015—in the school's history and the largest national crowd on record for a spring game. Weather contributed greatly to that; attendance has fluctuated considerably depending on the forecast, among other factors. Six years later, Ohio State lured 99,391 to Ohio Stadium, as fans had the chance to observe the team for the first time since it won the national championship.

When the weather cooperates, Ohio State has proven to be able to draw close to a sellout crowd for its annual Spring Game.

In Urban Meyer's first exhibition as head coach in 2012, 81,112 ventured to Ohio Stadium for the spring game, the most of any school in the nation. A year later, with Ohio Stadium undergoing renovations, the university shifted the game to Paul Brown Stadium in Cincinnati. There, the affair attracted 37,643 fans. Ohio State was headed for a similar drawing at the 2014 game—played back in the comfortable confines of Ohio Stadium—because of its ticket prices. Originally, the university asked for $20 for a ticket. That price dropped to $12 and, ultimately, $5. In the end, 61,058 passed through the turnstiles.

The Buckeyes practice for about three weeks before the annual spring game. It serves as a brief tune-up before summer arrives and dogged, two-a-day practices begin. Each coach has opted for a different method for choosing teams. Some have used captains. Others have split them up themselves. Sometimes it is Scarlet versus Gray. Others it is Offense versus Defense. There is usually something on the line. Often, some form of extra conditioning hangs in the balance. Quarterbacks typically sport a black jersey, deeming them safe from any tackling.

It is not the most thrilling, action-packed spectacle. Many fans exit the venue before the final whistle. It is, however, a breath of fresh air and a reminder of what lies ahead when the football season seems so far away. And, no matter the final score, Ohio State always wins.

· ·

Kenny G's Smooth Jazz

John Hicks played for some of the most heralded teams in Ohio State history. In his three seasons—1970, 1972, and 1973 (he missed the 1971 season because of an injury)—the Buckeyes amassed a 28–3 mark. So, he knows a little bit about successful squads. What, then, is the key to rattling off so many consecutive wins?

"You have to have a lot of luck," Hicks said. "You have to have some key people and keep them healthy."

Fortune is not promised, however. Otherwise, Braxton Miller would not have been bound to a stretcher en route to the hospital as Ohio State attempted to extend its winning streak in 2012.

For an October day in Columbus, it was a scorcher. It was one of those sweltering afternoons in which the imposing humidity forces perspiration from every pore upon one's first step outdoors. It was a 90-degree day reminiscent of summertime in Houston, the hometown of Kenny Guiton. On this balmy afternoon, Guiton was taking some coveted snaps and spewing his usual array of trash talk. Receiver Corey "Philly" Brown classified the verbal jabs as "rated R." He enjoyed prodding the Ohio State defense in practice with his taunts and sneers. Defensive tackle Michael Bennett said he simply laughed every time Guiton tossed a barb his way.

"He's not trying to cut deep," Bennett said. "He's not trying to make me question myself. We're just messing around in practice, trying to make it a little lighter. He's saying something and it's like, 'All right, now I have to sack him.'"

So with Miller headed for the hospital, Guiton was tasked with rescuing the Buckeyes from what would have been their first defeat under head coach Urban Meyer.

"Kenny is crazy," said Brown. "When he comes in the huddle, he's loud, obnoxious."

After heaving an interception late in the fourth quarter, Guiton engineered a last-minute, game-tying touchdown drive complete with a two-point conversion. He tossed the touchdown pass to his roommate, receiver Chris Fields, with three seconds remaining in regulation. He delivered the two-point toss to tight end Jeff

Heuerman. He then positioned Ohio State for an overtime score—a Carlos Hyde one-yard plunge into the end zone—that preserved the team's unblemished record.

"That changed a lot," Guiton said. "That changed a lot in my life."

A couple of years earlier, Guiton had consulted his inner circle about transferring away from Ohio State. A couple of years before that, he was an underwhelming recruit who appeared destined to attend Prairie View A&M. That one relief effort against the Boilermakers altered everything.

"I think that was the moment of his life when you can say it was like a grow-up stage," said Marlon Taplin-McMillan, Guiton's mentor and offensive coordinator in high school. "Sometimes you are put in certain situations where you don't know if you can do it or not. In that situation, being down and Braxton Miller gets hurt and now it's put on your shoulders to win this football game, it's make or break."

The following season, the Buckeyes elected eight captains. Guiton was selected as one of the eight. He was the only one not to own a starting job.

"I wonder how many times that's happened, the backup quarterback is elected captain and there's no real surprise internally," Meyer said.

Miller missed more time because of injuries in 2013 and Guiton thrived on the field. He set a school record with six touchdown passes in a 76–0 win against Florida A&M at Ohio Stadium. A week earlier, he threw for 276 yards and four touchdowns and rushed for 92 yards on the road against Cal, a game in which Ohio State prevailed 52–34. The fans, without hesitation, embraced him.

"Every time I run out onto the field," Guiton said, "it's a standing ovation and it just runs through my veins, a crazy feeling that I can't explain."

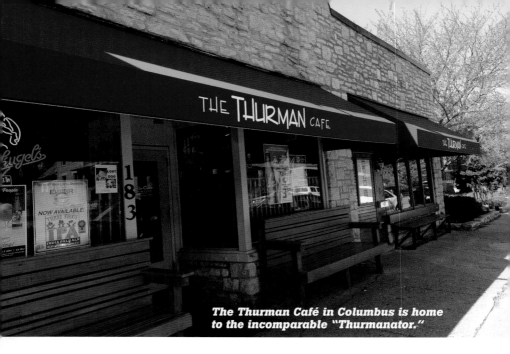

The Thurman Café in Columbus is home to the incomparable "Thurmanator."

Attempt to Eat the "Thurmanator"

WHERE: 183 Thurman Ave. in German Village, Columbus, Ohio, 43206

WHEN: 11:00 AM to 2:30 AM daily, though the full menu is served only until midnight Sunday through Thursday and until 1:00 AM on Fridays and Saturdays

HOW TO DO IT: Consume every last bite of the monstrous burger

COST FACTOR: $19.99 for the Thurmanator, the rest of the menu includes appetizers from $4-7 and wings, burgers, sandwiches, pizzas, salads, Coney dogs, subs, and gyros for $6-15

BUCKET RANK: 🪣 🪣 🪣

It all begins with the bottom bun. An innocent layer of mayo comes next. Then, a sheet of green lettuce, a slight, temporary reminder of what healthy eating looks like. A sliced red tomato and a few pickles follow. Atop that lie a handful of yellow banana peppers. Then, the first boulder on the mountainous spectacle. It is a 12-ounce, juicy beef patty. Strips of bacon, which are doused in cheddar cheese, rest atop the beef. Then, it is yet another 12-ounce burger patty. Nestled atop the meat are a smattering of sautéed mushrooms and onions. They are covered by a layer of ham. Streams of mozzarella and American cheese make the whole thing messy. The top bun seals off the monstrous concoction.

The Thurman Cafe, a Columbus landmark, offers much more than its claim to fame, the Thurmanator, a messy mass of meat, cheese, bread, and palate cleansers. The restaurant, owned since 1942 by generations of the Suclescy family, serves pizzas, sandwiches, wings, salads, Coney Island hot dogs, subs, and a litany of fried goodies, from pretzel bites to burrito bites to jalapeños to banana peppers to poblano peppers to pickles to portabella mushrooms.

The "Thurmanator" is a colossal burger, with layers of meat, cheese, and fixins.

The Travel Channel show *Man v. Food* host Adam Richman visited The Thurman Cafe in 2008. As he sat at his table, he was brought the Thurmanator. Upon visual contact with the beast of a burger, his eyes lit up and his mouth opened wide.

"Damn," was the first word out of his mouth. "That's, like, a Double Thurman?"

"No," the waitress replied. "That's just a Single Thurman."

Richman described the burger as such: "The flavor of the meat is awesome. The thing is, there is so much flavor going on. It's like a ham and cheese sandwich and it's a burger and it's a salad. Then in the middle, you get the onion blast, which is like a whole other thing. I actually applaud the messiness of it. I want to have a secondary mouth to attack it from underneath.

"The sheer size and tastiness of this burger blew me away."

· ·

Schooling the Opposition

Even the coach could not believe it.

"I've got my third-string quarterback sitting here to my left," said Urban Meyer. "I've never met a third-string quarterback [this good] before, and he's 3–0."

For two years, Cardale Jones was known around campus for a remark he made on Twitter, one that he came to regret. At least by the end of his third year at Ohio State, he could laugh at it. He finally had vindication. No longer was he defined by the quick, 140-character emission of frustration.

On October 5, 2012, Jones posted on his Twitter account: "Why should we have to go to class if we came here to play FOOTBALL, we ain't come to play SCHOOL, classes are POINTLESS."

Forget the biology lab or English essay. Meyer considered booting Jones from the team. There was more than the tweet, a message that did nothing but stir up a narrative about Ohio State's third-string quarterback and the motivations for college athletes.

"It wasn't pleasant his first year here," Meyer said.

Fast-forward 27 months. Jones hoisted the College Football Playoff championship trophy as he stood at the podium at AT&T Stadium in Arlington, Texas, the epicenter of the Buckeyes' implausible title run. After Braxton Miller and J.T. Barrett were shelved with injuries, Jones was summoned to guide Ohio State to its first championship in 12 years. The kid who had no interest in sitting through a European history lecture could now teach a course on teamwork.

"It was very tough, because being a No. 3 and then having two guys in front of you performing the way they were before Braxton and J.T. went down," Jones said. "It was tough to stay positive. It was tough to have that mind-set of 'I'm here for a reason.' But with the help of my teammates and my coaches, I got a chance to stick it out."

Finally, he was recognized for the right reasons. Everywhere he walked in Columbus, someone wanted to take a picture with him or request an autograph.

"I don't mind that," Jones said, "but it's still unreal right now, like, you really want my autograph or a picture with me? That's probably one of the strangest things. It happened so fast."

The week of the national championship game, Jones and a few teammates joined receivers coach Zach Smith at the hospital to visit a relative who had recently had open heart surgery. On his way out of the hospital, Jones was stopped by a nurse. A doctor in the hospital was a big fan of the 6'5" quarterback. The nurse and the doctor's friends asked Jones if he would surprise the doctor. Jones entered the room. The doctor cried.

"I'm like, 'Oh, snap,'" Jones said. "She was like my biggest fan and stuff, so that was pretty weird to see someone cry because they got a chance to meet me."

Jones made his first career start against Wisconsin in the Big Ten Championship Game. The Buckeyes cruised to a 59–0 victory. A month later, Jones directed Ohio State to a 42–35 win against Alabama in the Sugar Bowl. The week leading up to the national title game against Oregon, he blocked every number in his phone except those of his mother and Meyer. He was focused, fixated on excellence.

Jones and the Buckeyes captured that national championship and talk soon shifted to the quarterback's decision to return to school or depart early for the NFL. A college player with three starts under his belt and one month as anything other than the third-string quarterback was justifiably being linked to the professional ranks. He opted to stay in school.

"He's one of the most improved players I've ever been around," Meyer said.

Meyer routinely referred to Jones' growth as a fascinating case study. Even the coach could not believe the maturation of the man sitting to his left.

"If everybody wasn't aligned, that wouldn't be the same young man sitting right there," Meyer said. "His support at home, his high school coach, his position coach, they're all obviously close. Obviously Cardale bought in."

Buckeye Donuts is a staple near Ohio State's campus, as it sells donuts, coffee, and other treats 24 hours a day.

Stop in for a Donut from Buckeye Donuts

WHERE: The Corner of 18th and High Street, Columbus, Ohio, 43201

WHEN: 24 hours a day, seven days a week

HOW TO DO IT: Grab a donut to go, or stop in for some food

COST FACTOR: Donuts are 99¢ apiece

BUCKET RANK:

In 1969, a little donut shop opened in what is now the heart of High Street, adjacent to the center of Ohio State's campus. Today, the diminutive restaurant serves more than just sugary pastries. Buckeye Donuts offers gyros, chicken tenders, cheese fries, fried mushrooms, onion rings, mozzarella sticks, jalapeño poppers, hummus plates, salads, and breakfast sandwiches. Donuts remain the staple, but for a place open 24 hours a day, seven days a week, the variety lures customers of all types and at all times.

A sign with a miniature cartoon Brutus Buckeye, holding a donut as big as his body, hangs from the wall of the building. The cramped space has a corner of seats against a window to the left of the entrance. Straight ahead lie a wall full of donuts. To the right sits a U-shaped bar area and a row of seats against the main window. The inside is reminiscent of an old diner. Old men sit at the bar and dip their donuts into their coffee-filled mugs as they mouth the words to a late '80s/early '90s soundtrack that plays "She Drives Me Crazy" by the Fine Young Cannibals, "I'm Gonna Be (500 miles)" by the Proclaimers, and "(I've Had) the Time of My Life" by Bill Medley and Jennifer Warnes. Two small, flat-screen TVs show the news or the Ohio State game, depending on the time of day and day of the week.

As the clock ticks into after-hours, the location quickly fills with youngsters looking for a post-bar snack. In the morning, those en route to class or work swing by for a donut and a coffee. The place carries 32 varieties of donuts and all are made fresh daily. They sell donuts filled with vanilla cream, chocolate cream, Boston cream, lemon, blueberry, strawberry, apple spice, custard, jelly, and apple raspberry. Glazed donuts include honey dip, French cruller, red velvet, Devil's food, blueberry, and buttermilk. Cake donuts include old fashioned, powdered sugar, coconut, peanut, and cinnamon sugar. Each donut costs only 99 cents. The shop also offers apple fritters, cinnamon raised twists, muffins and cookies, and eclairs with white frosting, chocolate, and peanut butter. For those thirsting for a drink to complement a morning donut, the place serves orange, apple, cranberry, and grapefruit juice, as well as iced tea. They offer catering packages of donuts and coffee, too.

The eatery boasts that it has served the likes of legendary Ohio State football coach Woody Hayes, comedian Dave Attell, and musician Prince. Framed pictures of Hayes, former Ohio State coach Jim Tressel, and the downtown Columbus skyline hang from the walls. Also spotted among the vast collection of art are a photo of actor Marlon Brando on a motorcycle, a giant Star Wars poster, and pictures of the owner hard at work. A large, framed exhibit titled "Expressions by Rolando Giambelli" displays 26 album covers by The Beatles in order of their release. One cardboard poster reads "Drink Coffee: Do Stupid Things Faster With More Energy." Another one says "Coffee! If you're not shaking, you need another cup."

Study the Legacy of Chic Harley

Ohio State football was mired in a phase of mediocrity in the early 1900s. When Chic Harley, a highly sought after multisport high school athlete, opted for nearby Ohio State, rather than Notre Dame, Michigan, and Army, the program and the university changed course forever.

In 1916, Harley's sophomore year and first with the varsity squad, he led the Buckeyes to their first Big Ten championship with an undefeated season. Harley ran the ball, passed the ball, caught the ball, intercepted the ball, and even kicked the ball for Ohio State. His well-rounded play reflected his versatility, though that was common for elite athletes of that era.

"That was more the nature of the game back at that time," said Ohio State football historian Jack Park. "You played both ways and did everything. Usually your best athlete was your best runner or your best passer, and he was also your best punter. The game has become so specialized today that you've got specialists to come in and handle all of that now."

The unbeaten season placed Ohio State on the map in terms of rising athletic departments. Harley was honored as the school's first consensus first-team All-American, for which he later earned a plaque in Buckeye Grove outside of Ohio Stadium. His exemplary play on the field garnered the football program some national exposure.

"As far as the people who have really been the driving forces behind Ohio State football, Harley is the guy who got it started," Park said. "He brought national attention to Ohio State football."

For the first time, there was a buzz surrounding Buckeyes athletics. The local kid from East High School in Columbus generated excitement that attracted more and more fans. By the end of the 1916 campaign, capacity crowds routinely filed into undersized Ohio Field to watch Harley and the Buckeyes.

"He created, with his play on the field and his personality, this euphoria about football," said Todd Wessell, Harley's great-nephew.

By the end of the season, there was no more room at Ohio Field for the flocks of fans. The surge in attendance triggered the concept for a new football stadium. Harley used his prominence in Columbus to help raise money for the new venue. He was a quiet, soft-spoken man, but his presence alone convinced people to contribute to the university's development.

"When people were asked to donate, they would gladly reach into their pockets," Wessell said. "People would come out in large numbers, just because it was Chic Harley. He generated the euphoria so that people would enroll and give money to the university so they could hire better professors and have better athletic facilities. That was very important in developing Ohio State as it is today."

The plans for Ohio Stadium, which would open in 1922 and hold about 50,000 more fans, demonstrated another way in which Harley's Buckeyes revolutionized the football program at Ohio State. Park surmised that, prior to Harley's arrival, more people were attending some of the major high school games in the area than Ohio State's football affairs.

"Athletic director L.W. St. John saw this as a way to capitalize on that momentum, and eventually build a much bigger stadium," Park said.

Though the new stadium was erected after the conclusion of Harley's college career, larger crowds continued to show up each Saturday afternoon. Harley directed Ohio State to another undefeated season in 1917, at 8–0–1. He spent the next year fighting in World War I, but returned to Ohio State in 1919, when he led the Buckeyes to a 6–1 mark.

Ohio State—or any other football program—has rarely enjoyed a stretch of dominance on par with what Harley's bunch achieved. Harley's teams went 21–1–1 in three years with three Big Ten championships and in 1919, the Buckeyes defeated Michigan for the first time. Harley himself was a four-sport letterman and three-time All-American.

George Halas had to beg Harley to join the Decatur Staleys, the team that later became the Chicago Bears. Toward the end of the 1921 season, Harley began to suffer from a mental illness. The ailment derailed his career and led to his admittance to the Veteran's Administration Hospital in Danville, Illinois, where he spent the majority of the rest of his life.

Richard Wessell, Harley's nephew, was afraid that people would forget about the Ohio State icon. At times, Harley was healthy enough to visit his family in Chicago, Richard included. Harley died in 1974.

"My father was afraid that people at Ohio State would forget," Todd Wessell said. "People have forgotten. A lot of people don't know him.

Most people don't know anything about him, other than that he was a good football player. But he was so much more than that."

Wessell spoke highly of Harley's personality and his charm. He said Harley possessed the qualities "that most of us dream about, but don't really meet as human beings." Ohio State began retiring jersey numbers in 1999. Harley's No. 47 was finally memorialized in 2004. Park said the university could have done more to recognize "the guy that helped put Ohio State on the national map, probably more than any other player."

"It's not just the football player," Wessell said. "Ohio State has tons of great football players. There's only one Chic Harley."

Take a Walk through Buckeye Grove

In the winter, it looks like a barren wasteland, an arctic tundra lined with naked, leafless, lifeless trees. Snow covers up the bronze plaques at the base of each plant. In the summer, with the trees fully bloomed and able to provide shade for those sitting on the nearby benches, it is perhaps the most serene spot on campus. No matter the season, since 1934, the Buckeye Grove, outside of Ohio Stadium and Lincoln and Morrill Towers, has represented the best Ohio State football has had to offer over the years.

The path outside of the Horseshoe winds up a hill, overlooking tennis courts and an open field often used for soccer. At the entrance stands an archway, topped with red letters spelling out Buckeye Grove. A narrow path, with trees and benches on both sides, splits into two. At that juncture start the rows of trees and corresponding plaques

Each All-American in Ohio State football history has a tree planted in his honor on campus in Buckeye Grove.

honoring every All-American player in Ohio State football history. Each section of trees and mulch is lined with bricks. Those stretches of bricks are interrupted with blocks of cement. On each block rests a bronze outline of the state of Ohio, with an identifier for each award-winning player.

The history lesson begins with Boyd Cherry, named to the All-America team in 1914. His honor reads "Boyd Cherry, All America, 1914, Memorial Tree." Charles "Chic" Harley also has his distinction near the beginning. He was named an All-American in 1916, 1917, and 1919. In the center of the grove, grass separates the areas of mulch. In the mulch, the trees are lined in rows, two at a time. Other notable names on display in the area include halfback Vic Janowicz (1950), defensive back Jack Tatum (1969–70), linebacker Chris Spielman (1986–87), offensive tackle Orlando Pace (1995–96), and

HEISMAN WINNERS

Six Ohio State players have combined to win seven Heisman Trophy awards, given to the "outstanding college football player whose performance best exhibits the pursuit of excellence with integrity. Winners epitomize great ability combined with diligence, perseverance, and hard work," according to the Heisman Trust. The honor has been handed out each year since 1935, when Chicago's Jay Berwanger earned the distinction after rushing for 577 yards and six touchdowns.

Les Horvath, quarterback (1944)
Runner up: Glenn Davis, running back, Army
Horvath served as the quarterback in 1944, but he attempted only 32 passes all season. He rushed 163 times for 924 yards, an average of nearly six yards per carry. He totaled 12 touchdowns on the ground for the Buckeyes, who finished the season 9–0.

Vic Janowicz, quarterback (1950)
Runner up: Kyle Rote, running back, Southern Methodist
Janowicz was a jack of all trades for Ohio State. He played quarterback; he threw 12 touchdown passes. He ran the ball; he totaled 314 yards on the ground, with four touchdowns. He also kicked and punted.

Howard "Hopalong" Cassady, running back (1955)
Runner up: Jim Swink, running back, Texas Christian
Cassady won the award by the largest margin ever at the time. He rushed for 958 yards and 15 touchdowns for Woody Hayes' crew.

Archie Griffin, running back (1974)
Runner up: Anthony Davis, running back, USC
Griffin averaged 6.6 yards per carry during his junior season, as he amassed 1,695 yards on the ground and totaled 12 touchdowns for an Ohio State team that seemed primed for a national championship until a three-point loss at Michigan State in early November.

Archie Griffin, running back (1975)
Runner up: Chuck Muncie, running back, California
Griffin only scored four touchdowns and his rushing total—1,450 yards—was surpassed by the three running backs who finished immediately behind him in the Heisman Trophy balloting, but nevertheless, the senior captured his second straight piece of hardware, becoming the only two-time recipient.

Eddie George, running back (1995)
Runner up: Tommie Frazier, quarterback, Nebraska
George totaled 1,927 yards on the ground and 24 touchdowns for John Cooper's squad, which won its first 11 games before falling short at Michigan and against Tennessee in the Citrus Bowl. The vote was somewhat close, as Frazier directed the Cornhuskers to an undefeated season and national title. Nebraska won its 12 games by an average of 39 points per contest.

Troy Smith, quarterback (2006)
Runner up: Darren McFadden, running back, Arkansas
Smith won the Heisman Trophy in a landslide after he threw for 2,542 yards and 30 touchdowns while completing two-thirds of his pass attempts. He tossed only six interceptions and led the Buckeyes to the national championship game, where Ohio State sputtered for the first time all season.

linebacker Ryan Shazier (2013). Joey Bosa, an All-American in 2014, became the 187th player to earn that honor.

Ohio State considers any legitimate source for a player's inclusion into the arboral fraternity. In addition to the Associated Press, Football Writers Association of America, American Football Coaches Association, The Sporting News, and Walter Camp Football Foundation—all backed by the NCAA—the university counts publications such as ESPN.com, *USA Today*, and *Sports Illustrated*.

Trees are typically planted in a ceremony prior to the annual Spring Game. They were relocated to their current domain, near the southwest corner of Ohio Stadium, in 2001 because of renovations to the venue.

· ·

Life Goes On

During his coaching career, Jim Tressel preferred not to reflect on anything. Upon winning the 2002 national championship and upon beating Michigan nine times out of 10, he did not want to consider his place in Ohio State coaching history. He opted to save those thoughts for the day he was relegated to a rocking chair.

"The moment a game ends or the moment a season ends, the immediate next logical question by any media person or any coach or young person who is going to be returning to the squad the following year is, 'How are we going to be next year?'" Tressel said. "I have always said reflection is for the person who is not coaching anymore or who is not playing anymore. Just like a junior who is heading into his senior year is not going to spend much time reflecting. He's going to spend time thinking about that senior year. That's just the nature of what we do. You really don't reflect on that until it's over."

That mind-set helped him persevere through a few hiccups during his tenure at Ohio State, which ended amid an NCAA scandal in May 2011. Any time Tressel came across a less than desirable on-field result, he quickly shifted his focus to what stood before him.

"If we play a ball game I know we didn't play anywhere near to our capabilities, obviously that's disappointing," Tressel said. "But immediately, my thoughts go to, 'OK, what didn't we do well? Why didn't we do it well? What do we have to do to get the ship headed back in the right direction?' After you're done passionately working day by day, you might say, 'Oh, that Purdue game from '09 really bothered me,' or, 'That loss to Michigan in '03, we weren't ready. I didn't have them ready.'"

Troy Smith learned a lot from his college coach. That mentality Tressel employs rubbed off on his former quarterback. The last time Smith ever suited up for Ohio State, the Buckeyes were obliterated on the grandest stage in a humiliating 41–14 loss to Florida in the 2007 BCS Championship Game. Instead of sulking and chastising himself for completing only four of 14 pass attempts for 35 yards, he pushed his thinking forward.

"When you are going into a game and you lose this way, obviously you lost this way for a reason," Smith said. "You know, the spread and the score—who would have ever thought it would be like that? But there's not that much that you can really do about it. Life goes on."

The quarterback who demonstrated maturity in the face of disappointment came a long way in a few short years. Smith joined the Buckeyes on a scholarship for the 2002 season. He did not really have a position or a path to success.

"Troy came in here as an 'athlete,'" Tressel said. "We did not promise him he would be a quarterback. He kind of had to prove that he could. It wasn't easy for him at first and he didn't approach it the right way necessarily at first. He let it really affect him through the beginning of his career."

Smith redshirted during the 2002 campaign and primarily saw action as a kick returner in his freshman season. He entered the 2004 season as the backup quarterback before taking over the position when starter Justin Zwick suffered a shoulder injury. Smith won four of five games, but relinquished his grip on the starting role after he accepted $500 from a booster. He was suspended for the 2004 Alamo Bowl and the 2005 season opener against Miami (Ohio). He eventually regained his spot under center and never looked back, leading Ohio State to a 34–20 win against Notre Dame in the 2006 Fiesta Bowl and to a 12–0 regular-season record the following season.

He accounted for nearly 2,900 yards of offense in 2005, with 16 passing touchdowns and 11 rushing touchdowns. A year later, he totaled 2,542 yards through the air, completed 65 percent of his passes, and threw for 30 touchdowns with only six interceptions. Those statistics earned him the Heisman Trophy.

"To watch him grow to understand, 'OK, I know what it takes to be a quarterback. I know what I have to study, what I have to work on, what I have to be, what I have to get better at and I know the type of leader I need to be,'" Tressel said, "to see him five years later end up the Heisman Trophy winner when he didn't even come here to be a quarterback, or he did but we weren't sure—to me, that was very rewarding. Now, it was not without some consternation over the course of time, but it was fun to see at the end of the day."

Tressel said that type of mentoring and developing young adults was always his favorite part of coaching. He was able to continue a similar role when he transitioned to the academic side of collegiate employment once his tenure at Ohio State ended.

"Those days that I see progress in each of the young people or a particular young person, you see a lightbulb go on in someone's head or you see someone have a tough situation and then grow from it or handle it," Tressel said. "My highlight would be progress."

Tressel's reign with the Buckeyes ended on a sour note. He rode off into a tornado, not a sunset. Smith's did not end in ideal fashion, either, with the lopsided loss to Florida. But he had grown enough to know that that's how life operates at times. That's a message he learned from Tressel.

"You're not going to be able to do things and have a storybook ending all the time," Smith said. "That's life."

. . . .

Learn the Names of "Linebacker U"

O hio State has made a name out of producing elite linebackers. The Buckeyes have had nine linebackers selected in the first round of the NFL Draft. Here is a sampling of some of the star defenders to have sported scarlet and gray on Saturdays.

Ryan Shazier: Heart of Gold
Vernon Shazier was sitting in the stands at a football game when the name-calling started.

"Cue Ball." "Patch."

The insults were hurled at his son, Ryan, the boy with the irregularly covered scalp.

"Kids can just be cruel," Vernon said.

Over and over, Urban Meyer mentioned Christian Bryant's name after the safety suffered a broken ankle in late September of his senior season in 2013. When Meyer first spoke of the injury, after a win against Wisconsin, the coach pounded the podium in frustration. Bryant was the heart and soul of Ohio State's defense, the chief

Ryan Shazier was named an All-American in 2013, when he anchored the defense on an Ohio State team that went 12–2.

captain of a team once devoid of leaders. In the time it required to make a simple tackle in the waning moments of that game against the Badgers, Bryant was gone.

The Orange Bowl at the end of that season was supposed to have been Bryant's farewell, the last hurrah for the graduate of Glenville Academy in Cleveland. Meyer referred to him as Ohio State's "best player" on either side of the football. Someone had to step up, fill his shoes, and embrace the role of on-field commander. Someone had to ditch the business casual for the Superman cape. Shazier was prepared for the occasion.

For a while, the "Cue Ball" jabs, knocks at the mostly barren dome he sported in elementary school, took a toll on Shazier's self-esteem. He suffers from alopecia, an autoimmune disorder that causes hair loss. Eventually, with guidance from his parents, he brushed aside the taunting. Vernon helped his son craft a virtuous, altruistic temperament.

"My message is always to act like a champion," Vernon said.

In Meyer's eyes, Shazier excelled at leading and at undertaking the responsibility left up for grabs after doctors diagnosed Bryant's injury. Meyer said the linebacker did "a really magical job at that."

Vernon encourages people for a living. He has served as a pastor, a football coach, and a chaplain for the Miami Dolphins. He has provided motivational speeches for the Buckeyes. He met with a few Ohio State players in the days leading up to the Orange Bowl. It did not take long for Shazier's teammates to figure out where Ryan acquired his spirit.

"It has a lot to do with character and his upbringing," said linebacker Joshua Perry.

Meyer referenced Ohio State's 35–23 win at Penn State in 2012 as the game in which Bryant morphed into a leader. He said Bryant "took over the locker room, took over the team and, as a result, we had a heck of a game." That was also the game in which Shazier, then a freshman, donned a No. 48 jersey, a way of honoring Gary Curtis, the team manager of his high school in Plantation, Florida. Curtis succumbed to muscular dystrophy a few months earlier.

"That hurt a lot," Shazier said. "It made me really think about things. It made me think about life. You never know when it's your last game, your last play or your last day."

When Ohio State linebacker Curtis Grant returned home to Virginia following the death of his father in October 2013, Shazier pleaded with Meyer to permit him to follow his teammate east for support.

"When Ryan comes to me like that," Meyer said, "I'm like, 'Settle down. What's the best thing to do?' It's all pure—you know, pure ideas and caring in its pure form, which is kind of cool."

Shazier wore Bryant's No. 2 jersey for the remainder of the season after the defensive back underwent surgery.

"The stuff he does just lets you know that he cares about his teammates," said defensive lineman Michael Bennett. "Everyone knows that his number is going to be seen a lot, so grabbing Christian Bryant's number just makes sure people still remember No. 2."

Scrawled across Shazier's left arm is a Bible verse, Philippians 4:13, which reads: "I can do all things through Christ who strengthens me."

"All my life, people have been helping me in all types of situations," Shazier said. "It's only right to pay it back. When you need help, it's only right to help others."

He helped plenty on the field during his three years at Ohio State. As a junior in 2013, he totaled 134 tackles, six sacks, and four forced fumbles. As a sophomore, he logged 115 tackles, five sacks, and three forced fumbles. Perry said Shazier took pride "in being a good guy off the field and being a monster on the field." That reputation helped him become the 15th overall selection in the 2014 NFL Draft by the Pittsburgh Steelers.

He played his final game with the Buckeyes in south Florida, not far from his hometown, where, Vernon said, "he experienced the good side and the dark side, the bad side. He experienced, he saw, he felt what it's like when people say things about you, when people mistreat you."

There was no heckling and no name-calling at the Orange Bowl. In fact, close to 100 of Shazier's friends and family members sat in the stands at Sun Life Stadium. There was plenty of support for the kid with the wide smile who has doled out support at every opportunity presented to him.

"He's one of the most incredible young men I've ever been around," Meyer said. "He's got a heart of gold."

Marcus Marek: The Standard

For three consecutive years, Marcus Marek led the Buckeyes in tackles. By the time he graduated from Ohio State, he had become the program's all-time leading tackler, with 572. He was named a consensus All-American in 1982. Marek was named the player of the game in Ohio State's 24–14 win on Senior Day against Michigan, as he totaled 19 tackles and set up the Buckeyes' clinching score with an interception. Ohio State forced six turnovers that afternoon against the Big Ten champions, as head coach Earle Bruce said the unit played with "enthusiasm and intensity. They gave a great effort today. There was a lot of great hitting.

"I was never so proud of a team in my life. Defensively, Marek was outstanding."

Tom Cousineau: Stat Stuffer

You can find Tom Cousineau's name scattered all throughout the Ohio State record books. He ranks tied for first with 29 tackles in a single game and holds the record with 211 tackles in 12 games in 1978. He owns five of the top 10 places on the leaderboard for most tackles in a single game. Overall, he checks in three tackles shy of Marcus Marek's record of 572 for a career. In 1977, he was chosen as the Most Valuable Player of the Orange Bowl. He was named an All-American in 1977 and 1978, and was selected as Ohio State's MVP in his senior season. He became the first Ohio State player chosen first overall in the NFL Draft.

Chris Spielman: Heart and Soul

Chris Spielman might have produced the most decorated career of any linebacker in program history. He saved his best for the proper moments, too. Spielman—not the most imposing character, at about six feet and 247 pounds—tallied a school record–tying 29 tackles in the 1986 Michigan game, a contest in which the Buckeyes fell short 26–24 after a last-gasp field-goal attempt misfired. A year later, he merited the Lombardi Award, given to the nation's top lineman or linebacker. At the end of that season, his last in Columbus, he helped

BAIT AND TACKLE

There has been plenty of competition on the Ohio State historical leaderboard when it comes to tackling. The Buckeyes have had their share of elite linebackers. Here is a sampling of some of the top defensive performers in program history.

Most total tackles in a career:
1. Marcus Marek: 572 (1979–82)
2. Tom Cousineau: 569 (1975–78)
3. Chris Spielman: 546 (1984–87)
4. Steve Tovar: 408 (1989–92)
5. A.J. Hawk: 394 (2002–05)
6. Pepper Johnson: 379 (1982–85)
7. James Laurinaitis: 375 (2005–08)
8. Alvin Washington: 345 (1977–80)
9. Ed Thompson: 338 (1974–76)
10. Glen Cobb: 336 (1979–82)

Most total tackles in a single season:
1. Tom Cousineau: 211 (1978)
2. Chris Spielman: 205 (1986)
3. Marcus Marek: 178 (1982)
4. David Adkins: 172 (1977)
5. (tie) Chris Spielman: 156 (1987)
   Rowland Tatum: 156 (1983)
7. Ed Thompson: 149 (1976)
8. Marcus Marek: 148 (1981)
9. Tom Cousineau: 147 (1976)
10. Alvin Washington: 146 (1978)

Most total tackles in a single game:
1. (tie) Chris Spielman: 29 (1986)
   Tom Cousineau: 29 (1978)
3. Tom Cousineau: 28 (1978)
4. (tie) David Adkins: 24 (1977)
   Arnie Jones: 24 (1972)
6. (tie) Tom Cousineau: 23 (1978)
   Tom Cousineau: 23 (1975)
8. (tie) Chris Spielman: 22 (1986)
   Tom Cousineau: 22 (1976)
   Randy Gradishar: 22 (1973)

Most quarterback sacks in a career:
1. Mike Vrabel: 36 (1993–96)
2. Jason Simmons: 27.5 (1990–93)
3. Matt Finkes: 25 (1993–96)
4. Eric Kumerow: 23 (1984–87)
5. Vernon Gholston: 22.5 (2004, 2006–07)
6. Will Smith: 22 (2000–03)
7. Joey Bosa: 21 (2013–14)
8. John Simon: 20.5 (2009–12)
9. (tie) Brent Johnson: 18 (1997–00)
   Na'il Diggs: 18 (1997—99)

Most quarterback sacks in a single season:
1. Vernon Gholston: 14 (2007)
2. Joey Bosa: 13.5 (2014)
3. Mike Vrabel: 13 (1995)
4. (tie) Andy Katzenmoyer: 12 (1996)
   Mike Vrabel: 12 (1994)
6. Matt Finkes: 11 (1994)
7. (tie) Will Smith: 10.5 (2003)
   Jason Simmons: 10.5 (1991)
9. (tie) A.J. Hawk: 9.5 (2005)
   Mike Kudla: 9.5 (2005)

the Ohio State defense secure a 23–20 win against Michigan and carried head coach Earle Bruce off the field in what proved to be Bruce's final game as Buckeyes boss. Spielman was named the team's Most Valuable Player for that season.

Spielman was a two-time All-American who racked up more solo tackles (283) than any other player in Ohio State history. He totaled 546 tackles in all, third all-time, and 11 interceptions. He finished 10th in the balloting for the Heisman Trophy in 1986 and sixth in 1987. The Detroit Lions selected him in the second round of the 1988 NFL Draft. He was elected to the College Football Hall of Fame in 2009.

Randy Gradishar: "The Best"

If Woody Hayes refers to someone as the best player at a particular position that he ever coached, that player must have done something right. Randy Gradishar was twice named an All-American and finished sixth in the Heisman Trophy voting in 1973, when the Buckeyes finished the season with a 10–0–1 record that included a stretch of four shutouts in five games. On October 6, 1973, Gradishar registered 22 tackles in a 27–3 win against Washington State. He totaled 320 tackles during his tenure in Columbus. The Denver Broncos drafted him with the 14th overall selection in 1974. He was elected to the College Football Hall of Fame in 1998.

Steve Tovar: Tackling Machine

For three consecutive years (1990, 1991, 1992), Steve Tovar led Ohio State in tackles. He ranks fourth in program history in total tackles. He was named Big Ten Defensive Player of the Year as a senior in 1992, when he also served as the Ohio State co-captain, along with quarterback Kirk Herbstreit. Tovar was elected to the Ohio State Varsity O Hall of Fame in 2001. He was a third-round draft choice by the Cincinnati Bengals in 1993.

Andy Katzenmoyer: The Hulk

Some freshman showed up at Ohio Stadium sporting a No. 45 jersey, a number that had been on ice since two-time Heisman Trophy winner Archie Griffin donned it while running wild on opposing defenses. Andy Katzenmoyer did not take long to prove he could handle the heightened expectations that came with wearing such divine digits. The 6'4" behemoth became the first true freshman to start at linebacker in the season opener for Ohio State and he registered 12 sacks and 23 tackles for loss in his rookie year of 1996. After his 1997 season, the physically imposing linebacker earned the Butkus Award—the first Ohio State player to win the prestigious honor, given to the nation's top linebacker annually since 1985—and was a consensus first-team All-American. The New England Patriots made him a first-round NFL Draft pick in 1999.

Matt Wilhelm: The Centerpiece

On a stingy defensive unit littered with an abundance of NFL talent, Matt Wilhelm was right in the middle. In Ohio State's double-overtime upset of heavily favored Miami in the national championship game on January 3, 2003, Wilhelm led the Buckeyes with 11 tackles. That season, the middle linebacker totaled 19.5 tackles for loss, seventh-most in a season in program history. His 43.5 tackles for loss in his college career rank seventh in school history. He was an All-American in 2002 and was also named first-team All-Big Ten.

A.J. Hawk: The Ballhawk

As Jim Tressel's Buckeyes journeyed to a 14–0 record in 2002, A.J. Hawk chipped in a few tackles here and there on special teams. Ohio State captured the national title, a dominant defense graduated a handful of seniors, and Hawk joined the starting lineup at linebacker. He then proceeded to complete one of the most illustrious careers of any defensive player in school history. Hawk racked up 394 tackles while at Ohio State, the fifth-highest total in Buckeyes lore. His 41 tackles for loss rank eighth all-time. He also totaled 15 sacks and seven interceptions.

Hawk was chosen to the All-Big Ten first team on three occasions and was a first-team All-American in both 2004 and 2005. He was given the Lombardi Award and the Jack Lambert Trophy—awarded to the top collegiate linebacker—in 2005. At the end of that season, Ohio State bested Notre Dame 34–20 in the Fiesta Bowl. Hawk was named the Defensive Most Valuable Player of the game after he tallied nine tackles—including 3.5 for a loss—and two sacks of Fighting Irish quarterback Brady Quinn, his future brother-in-law. The Green Bay Packers selected Hawk with the fifth overall pick in the 2006 NFL Draft.

James Laurinaitis: Little Animal

James Laurinaitis started alongside A.J. Hawk in one game, Ohio State's Fiesta Bowl victory against Notre Dame following the 2005 regular season. He played in every game as a freshman that year, but beginning in 2006, he took on the role Hawk had played as the anchor and leader of the Silver Bullets. Laurinaitis led Ohio State in

James Laurinaitis was a three-time All-American linebacker before moving on to the NFL.

tackles and interceptions as a sophomore and he merited the Bronko
Nagurski Trophy given to the nation's best defensive player. After his
sophomore, junior, and senior seasons, Laurinaitis—nicknamed the
"Little Animal," after his father, John, a professional wrestler who
went by the ring name "Road Warrior Animal"—was named first-
team All-Big Ten and first-team All-America. He was handed the Jack
Lambert Trophy and the Butkus Award after the 2007 campaign. He
finished his collegiate career with 375 tackles.

Marcus Freeman: Heartbroken

Marcus Freeman has a big heart. He just never knew that it would
cost him his dream. In April 2009, Freeman waited patiently until
the fifth round of the NFL Draft to hear his name called. With a
professional career on the horizon, the former Ohio State linebacker
had achieved something he had worked toward for years.

"That I had a chance to play in the NFL was a great feeling," Freeman
said. "A dream come true."

One year later, that dream was over.

Freeman bounced around the league during his rookie campaign.
The Chicago Bears drafted him with the 154th overall pick, but
released him a week before the start of the regular season. Freeman
latched on with Buffalo and then with Houston, but both teams cut
him loose. When Freeman met with doctors in February 2010 for a
physical before he could join the Indianapolis Colts, his career path
was altered forever. Doctors discovered that Freeman had an enlarged
heart valve of the left ventricle.

"They said they couldn't pass me and they said that they're very sure
that no one else in the NFL will pass me," Freeman said.

The native of Huber Heights, Ohio, started at linebacker for the
Buckeyes for three seasons. He was named second-team All-Big Ten
during his last two years in scarlet and gray. He finished his collegiate

career 19th on the program's all-time tackle list. But in a matter of seconds, a man who said he felt completely healthy had to call it quits.

"I was devastated that I couldn't play the game anymore," Freeman said. "With this heart condition, it's bigger than football. You need to make sure you stay on top of it. That was the deciding factor that that was the end of my playing days."

Freeman said the doctors never speculated about what could have happened had the heart issue not been uncovered when it was. They did mention that one of their former patients, an athlete, had a similar condition that was not caught in time and he had to get emergency surgery.

"They didn't really get into detail about what could have happened, but they said it was dangerous," Freeman said. "I'm glad they found out before something bad happened and they found out that way."

At 24, Freeman's professional career was over. He had to find a new job, a new dream. Never could he have imagined that he would be mapping out his post-playing career so soon. But once he agreed with doctors that his days anchoring defenses were over, he immediately targeted a homecoming at Ohio State.

"He didn't pout about it," said James Laurinaitis, Freeman's old teammate in Columbus. "He went right to the people he needed to go to to continue what he wanted to do."

Freeman joined Ohio State's staff as a graduate assistant and defensive quality control coach. He worked directly with linebackers coach Luke Fickell. Right away, he revised his goals. He altered his aspirations. Instead of playing in the NFL and winning a Super Bowl, he wanted to be a head coach and an athletic director one day.

When Ohio State receivers coach Darrell Hazell took over as head coach at Kent State in 2011, he brought Freeman along as linebackers coach. Hazell became Purdue's head coach in 2013 and Freeman followed along in his same role. Having a big heart might have cost

Freeman his playing career, but it might have been a blessing in disguise.

"He's comfortable with it," Laurinaitis said. "He can't control the size of his heart. I told him that now he can tell his wife that he has an abnormally big heart and she should be thankful."

Meet Brutus Buckeye

One of the most recognizable mascots in sports, Brutus Buckeye once existed as an unsightly blob of paper mache. Two Ohio State students suggested the school use a buckeye for a mascot in 1965. The original thought was to lug a buck deer into Ohio Stadium, but that concept was nixed. Instead, the paper mache product debuted at Ohio State's homecoming game that year. It had large eyes, a small mouth, and bushy, white eyebrows and fit over a person's head and torso.

A couple of weeks later, it was refined into a 40-pound fiberglass figure with a friendlier face—except when the team was trailing, as it could flip its smile upside down. At that time, it finally received a name: Brutus, the winning entry in a campus-wide contest. At first, the mascot was operated by the Block "O" cheering section at the stadium. Eventually, that responsibility was transferred to the athletic department.

For two games in 1975, Brutus became just a small head that rested on a person's shoulders. The mascot's face featured a squinting eye and evil grin. It was swiftly replaced by the fiberglass getup. In 1977, the costume morphed into a smaller but heavier version. This Brutus sported a baseball cap with a scarlet "O". It was deemed too cumbersome for the performer to wear, so in the '80s, the uniform

Brutus Buckeye is a university icon, with his striped shirt and large, round head.

transformed again. At that point, it became just a Brutus head, worn on the shoulders of someone donning a scarlet and gray striped shirt with his name on the front and "00" on the back. The ensemble includes nine parts: the five-pound head, shirt, pants, belt, socks, shoes, gloves, wristband, and a white towel that dangles from the waistband. A gray hat with a scarlet brim and "O" sits atop the center of the head. It is the cap legendary coach Woody Hayes wore during the first game he ever coached at Ohio State in 1951.

Brutus, inducted into the Mascot Hall of Fame in 2007, makes more than 500 appearances each year. His trademark move is to do a headstand and spell out O-H-I-O with his legs. From where did the mascot derive such athleticism? He once starred in an ESPN commercial in which he performed aerobics with *SportsCenter* anchors under the instruction of renowned exercise enthusiast Richard Simmons. Brutus is the lone member of the class to collapse at the end of the commercial.

Brutus on Parade

In 2008, Ohio State's campus was overrun by mascots. A different version of Brutus Buckeye seemingly stood on nearly every corner of town.

Twenty people or organizations designed 40 statues—each about seven feet tall—of the university's chief nut. The statues stood atop a 2,000-pound cement base and were initially placed on the plaza outside of the Schottenstein Center, which served as a home base of sorts for the project. The figures were on display through the summer and fall and then a sponsor decided on the ultimate location for each. Many ended up at various spots on or near campus.

MASCOT MADNESS

Brutus Buckeye has had his share of run-ins with danger. He is not afraid of engaging in battle.

On September 18, 2010, Ohio State hosted Ohio University at the Horseshoe. As the band marched off the field and Brutus directed the football team onto it, the Bobcats' mascot, Rufus, raced onto the field and attempted to tackle Brutus, but missed. Rufus fell to the ground and Brutus raised his arms in confusion before he turned around and continued his trot toward the north end zone.

Rufus would not quit, however. He wiggled his way past the players and leapt onto Brutus' back in the end zone and began wailing away at the giant mascot head. He dragged him to the ground and got in one final punch as the two stood back up before security pulled Rufus away. Throughout the entire ordeal, the band continued to play, the cheerleaders continued to cheer, and the players continued their pre-game prayer—all while surrounding the fracas. Rufus raised his hands to taunt the crowd as he was escorted away. Brutus placed his hands on his hips, puzzled as to why Rufus had initiated the scrum.

The person in the Rufus costume, a student at another Ohio school, admitted after the fact that his original goal in auditioning for the position was to eventually tackle Brutus. He was relieved of his duties.

That has not been the only attack on Ohio State's most well-known nut.

During a spring practice in April 2013, Brutus entered the fray for an offensive play. When he got the ball, linebacker David Perkins leveled him with a punishing tackle. Brutus shakily returned to his feet and exited the field of play, but was not seriously harmed. Perkins showed little remorse, describing his pursuit as "see ball, get ball." He did wish Brutus well after the fact. Photo evidence of the play displays Perkins, head down and helmet nestled into Brutus' shoulder, using proper technique. Poor Brutus, however, did not have the benefit of any padding or protection. He was not wearing the black jersey that makes a player off-limits for tackling during practices.

As seems to be the trend, though, Brutus was again the last one standing. Perkins transferred schools less than two months later.

The money raised via each statue's sponsor contributed to the funding for renovations of the William Oxley Thompson Memorial Library, positioned in the center of campus, adjacent to The Oval. Each sponsor committed between $10,000 and $20,000. The statues began as 150-pound fiberglass sculptures. Then, the designers flexed their creative muscles.

Each version of Brutus has the mascot with his left hand on his hip and right arm extended high in the air. Here is a breakdown of each statue.

Adventure Brutus: Lasso in his right hand, extended high in the air, this one sports a 5 o'clock shadow, a cowboy hat, a fanny pack, and a gun in a holster. He stands with his legs apart while wearing a ragged white shirt and khaki pants.

Alumni Brutus: This statue portrays the simplicities of college. Items such as an Ohio State football jersey, a chalkboard with a scientific formula on it, and a computer monitor adorn a colorful, albeit hideous, one-piece outfit that no human being should ever don in public.

Archie Brutus: A representation of two-time Heisman Trophy winner Archie Griffin, a running back for the Buckeyes in the 1970s, this sculpture shows Brutus in a scarlet No. 45 uniform, with gray football pants, leg pads, and cleats. The base is painted green to represent football turf.

The "Archie Brutus" depicts legendary Ohio State running back Archie Griffin, in his No. 45 uniform.

Barnstormer Brutus: His eyes are aimed upward, peering into the sky. He sports a brown leather jacket with an Ohio State scarf draped over his left shoulder. The base is light blue with white clouds.

Basketball Brutus: This one wears a white basketball jersey and shorts, with high white socks.

Bill Willis Brutus: Similar to the Archie Brutus, this one honors Willis, a defensive lineman for Ohio State in the early 1940s and the Cleveland Browns for eight years after that. He wears a white No. 99 uniform on the front and a No. 30 Browns jersey on the back.

Blarney Brutus: His left eye closed in a wink, the Irish version of the mascot is clad in a green and gold tuxedo, white gloves, gold striped pants, and black and gold shoes as he stands atop a gold and green base. A little black and green leprechaun hat with a gold square tops his wide head.

Brainy Brutus: The smartest of the statues, this nerd sports black glasses and a graduation cap and gown as he hovers over textbooks and a calculator.

Break a Leg Brutus: Dressed as the Phantom of the Opera, with a white mask covering half of his face and a large, black hat adorning his head, this Brutus holds a rose in his right hand and wears a black leather trench coat and pants, as a candle and play program sit at his feet.

Butter Brutus: The statue of highest caloric content, the entire figure is painted the color of butter. Ironically, this sculpture was designed by the Central Ohio Chapter of the Huntington's Disease Society of America.

Christopher Columbus Brutus: The explorer wears a white button-down with a black leather skirt of sorts and a black hat.

Coach Tressel Brutus: Depicting former Ohio State head coach Jim Tressel, this statue has Brutus in a red sweater vest and black pants. He is wearing a headset and standing over a Buckeyes football helmet.

Cookie Baker Brutus: Sporting a white chef's hat, this Brutus is holding a box of his homemade treats while standing above a handful of chocolate peanut butter Buckeye sweets.

Dave Thomas Brutus: Representing the founder of Wendy's, who opened the first installment of his fast-food empire in Columbus, this Brutus dons a white-and-blue striped apron and cap, thin glasses, a white shirt, and red tie, and holds a spatula as he stands atop a base painted red and yellow, the colors that accompany the long-standing establishment.

Doctor Brutus: Clad in a white coat sporting the Ohio State medical center logo and teal scrubs, this Brutus holds a stethoscope and stands behind a replica model of DNA.

Dot the "I" Brutus: This Brutus depicts a band member, carrying his bulky brass instrument on his back and holding his hat high in the air as he prepares to complete the most renowned tradition in Ohio State lore.

Drum Major Brutus: Dressed in tight leather clothes and a tall, feathery cap, this Brutus holds a baton in his right hand.

First Buckeye in Space Brutus: This astronaut is prepared to launch into orbit in his spacesuit. The base is painted black with white stars and a depiction of Earth from a distance.

**The "Drum Major Brutus"
resembles a member of the Ohio
State Marching Band, with a baton
in his right hand.**

Fore Brutus: A set of golf clubs draped over his right shoulder, this Brutus sports a tacky wardrobe fit for the game, with a plaid cap, a yellow shirt with an Ohio State logo, brown pants, and scarlet and gray socks. His golf shoes settle into the green-painted base as he stands above the hole.

Freedom Brutus: The most patriotic of the bunch, this statue is wearing light brown camouflage and has an American flag draped over his shoulder.

Gogh Brutus: The artist rendition received an artistic design himself, with an orange beard and eyebrows, a teal smock with a couple of paintbrushes in his pocket, and a palette in his left hand. He stands atop Vincent Van Gogh's famous painting, *The Starry Night*. Of course, though Brutus does not have ears, this sculpture has hair covering the side of his face where the missing organ would be noticeable.

Gordon Gee Brutus: Gee, twice the president of the university, was known for his affinity for bow ties. This Brutus sports an oversized one, bright red in color, as he carries an Ohio State flag and wears Gee's patented glasses.

Green Brutus: It is neither the Boogeyman nor the Incredible Hulk. It is just Brutus, covered from head to toe in green shrubbery.

Hail, Brutus: This mascot wears a red and white toga with sandals and an Ohio State hat. Et tu, Brutus?

International Brutus: His shirt and shoes are covered with flags of the world's different nations and he stands atop a base painted like a globe.

Justice Brutus: Painted the color of cement, this Brutus is blindfolded, grips a sword in his left hand, and holds an old-fashioned scale in his right.

Liberty Brutus: A replica of the Statue of Liberty, just with a nut for a head.

Luv & Peace Brutus: A hippie with shaggy hair, a thin mustache, vibrant, flower-filled clothing, a peace-sign necklace, and flip flops. Groovy.

Mad Hatter Brutus: The *Alice in Wonderland* character wears a green and fuchsia top hat and matching bow tie. His buck teeth are impossible to ignore. He stands in a flower bed.

Mild-Mannered Reporter Brutus: This Brutus sports a black leather outfit with a light blue Superman shirt underneath, only a red "O" has replaced the superhero's traditional "S".

Mime Brutus: The quietest of the group, this sculpture has a white face, black beret, red suspenders, and a white-and-black striped shirt. This statue has never spoken.

Ole! Brutus: This matador is dressed in bright yellow, red, and black, with a black tie and sharp mustache.

Papa Brutus: Wearing glasses, a small black cap, and a brown sweater, this Brutus hovers over a collection of old, black-and-white photographs.

Pizza Chef Brutus: Somehow this Brutus holds up a pan of pizza with only his right index finger. This character wears a white chef's hat and has a curly mustache.

Rock n' Roll Brutus: This rocker wears an unbuttoned white and red shirt with white pants and a gold belt with an Ohio State emblem as he stands above a gold star with a red "O".

EXTRA POINTS

Breaking Brutus

"Dot the 'I' Brutus" stands outside of the College Traditions store on West Lane Ave. near Ohio State's campus, on display for all who walk past the shop that primarily sells school gear. Late one night—technically the early morning—in September 2011, an inebriated individual interrupted the statue's sleep. Three people took pictures with the statue as the clock pushed 2:30 AM. One male from the group then wrapped his hands around the statue and tried to pick it up, to no avail. He slapped Brutus' head a few times and ultimately yanked the hat off of the statue. The man will likely never be invited to dot the "I" at the Horseshoe.

Safety First Brutus: Caution is of utmost importance to this sculpture, which sports a red hard hat and gloves, a yellow vest that says "safety first," and yellow fireman boots as he stands in a construction site.

Super Fan Brutus: An avid Buckeyes supporter, dressed in a black OSU hat, red OSU sweatshirt, and a Buckeyes necklace as he holds an OSU flag and pom-poms, stands above a football, basketball, baseball, and softball.

Superhero Brutus: Clad in a red and white leather outfit, black cape and goggles, he is the guy to call in the event of an emergency.

Tin Brutus: The Tin Man from *The Wizard of Oz*, but with a wide, round head.

Woody Hayes Brutus: A representation of the longtime Ohio State football coach, this Brutus sports a white, short-sleeve button-down and red tie, with black pants, a whistle, glasses, and a black Ohio State hat.

Chapter 3

Ohio State—Michigan Rivalry

The Game

Whether undefeated or winless, it's still Ohio State–Michigan. They clashed in 2006 as the unbeaten No. 1 and No. 2 teams in the nation. Any sensible observer could have grasped the magnitude of the stakes. They have met in other years with little else on the line except for rivalry pride, which might be the most desired feature of the annual meeting anyway. The two schools, separated by about 180 miles, have dashed each other's national title hopes on numerous occasions.

Michael Bennett did not hold much ill will toward Michigan, despite growing up an hour southwest of Ohio State. Even during his freshman season as a Buckeye, he had yet to comprehend the intricacies of the rivalry. Then, the Buckeyes filtered out of the tunnel at Michigan Stadium in Ann Arbor, Michigan, and fans clad in blue greeted them by waving dollar bills, a reference to the NCAA violations that cost Ohio State its head coach, quarterback, and 12 wins from the 2010 season.

Bennett figured it out quickly. That is when he "bought in," he said. There is no love lost between the schools. There is a reason why every "M" is crossed out on campus in Columbus one week each year, why former Michigan coach Brady Hoke refused to refer to the university as anything other than "Ohio," and why Urban Meyer will say "our rival" or "the team up north" when referring to the Wolverines.

That made the 2011 loss in Ann Arbor—a 40–34 defeat in which Ohio State clutched a halftime lead—all the more insufferable for Bennett and his teammates.

"It was heartbreaking," said safety C.J. Barnett. "We let the great state of Ohio down."

The defeat snapped Ohio State's seven-game winning streak against Michigan and it sunk the Buckeyes as low as they had been, record-wise, since 1999. Ohio State finished the season with a 6–7 showing, its worst record since 1988.

"After that game, everybody was kind of just like, 'Man, we haven't lost to these guys in forever,'" said center Corey Linsley. "There were classes that went through and never lost."

Ohio State rebounded in 2012 to complete its 12–0 season. Payback did not enter into the minds of the players, though. There is no need for vengeance when the stakes of The Game are as high as can be, regardless of record, recent history, or anything else.

"As far as owing people and all that, that's not as important as the game itself," said offensive tackle Jack Mewhort. "The history and the tradition is so rich with this one that every year is a new year and you just want to win the one in front of you."

Ohio State's seven-game winning streak against Michigan, which spanned from 2004 to 2010, was the rivalry's longest since Michigan rattled off nine consecutive victories from 1901 to 1909.

When Ohio State and Michigan meet every year, something is on the line, be it a spot in the conference championship, an undefeated record, or, perhaps most importantly, rivalry pride.

"We might have taken them for granted thinking that Ohio State had won seven years straight," Bennett said.

Players at Ohio State are educated not to think that way. Granted, Bennett was a freshman at the time. He had yet to experience everything that comes with Michigan Week in Columbus, from the Mirror Lake jump to the football team treating every inch of Columbus outside of the Woody Hayes Athletic Center—where the players study film and practice—like a nuclear disaster area.

Whether undefeated or winless, it's still Ohio State–Michigan. Anyone involved in the unparalleled rivalry can find grounds for motivation.

"There's a reality in life that if you take anything for granted, you're probably not thinking right," said former Ohio State coach Jim Tressel. "We talk about a lot of things that we shouldn't take for granted. Maybe some things that aren't even that real to us. But when you talk about the Ohio State–Michigan game, that's very real."

Tressel coached the Buckeyes to victory in nine of his 10 meetings with the conference adversary.

"I've known before I was even part of the series of the significance of the game and the excitement of the game," Tressel said. "It's part of you if you like football and you're from Ohio State or you're from Michigan, or if you're in the Big Ten. You just grow up knowing that we're fortunate to be a part of this game. It's extraordinary."

The teams have traditionally clashed in the final week of the regular season.

"The nice thing of the Ohio State–Michigan game is it's always, 'Let it all hang out, because this is it,'" Tressel said. "It's Ohio State–Michigan. I'm sure you could talk to some people who have participated in this game as a player or a coach and they could tell you that, probably in the forefront of their mind of their memories of their time here, more so is the Ohio State–Michigan things that flow through their head than it is which bowl did you go to and where were you ranked and this and that."

HISTORY OF "THE GAME"

Ohio State and Michigan first squared off on October 16, 1897, in Ann Arbor, Michigan. The Wovlerines won that contest 36–0. They met again and ended in a scoreless tie in 1900. The teams then clashed each season through 1912. It took until the sixth contest for Ohio State to get on the scoreboard. In 1902, Michigan thumped the Buckeyes 86–0. In the first nine meetings, Michigan outscored Ohio State by a 278–6 margin. The Buckeyes did not defeat Michigan until the teams played in 1919, the 16th encounter between the two schools. In the first 15 matchups, Michigan outscored Ohio State by a 371–21 margin.

The teams have met each year since 1918, when Michigan rejoined the Western Conference, which eventually became the Big Ten. Ohio State prevailed in 1919, 1920, and 1921 before Michigan rattled off six straight victories. That remained the longest winning streak in the series until Jim Tressel's bunch emerged triumphant in each meeting from 2004 to 2010, though the 2010 win was later vacated. From 1934 to 1937, the Buckeyes notched four straight victories by a combined score of 114–0. In addition to the 1900 tie, the teams locked horns in 1910, 1941, 1949, 1973, and 1992.

One school of thought at the two schools suggests that there are three seasons: spring football, regular-season football, and the Ohio State–Michigan game.

"This game is as big for them as it is for us," said former Michigan coach Bo Schembechler. "We play in the last game of the year against these guys. If you total up the Big Ten Championships, it's usually one or the other. It goes way, way back. I know them on both ends because I knew who they were and everything. I just don't see one any bigger than this."

Cross out M's

The thirteenth letter of the alphabet is an oft relied-upon fixture in the English language. Occasionally, however, loyalty and pride precede convenience. As is the case whenever Ohio State and the school that resides in Ann Arbor in the state a bit north of Buckeyeland, the one with blue and yellow as its central colors, clash in the annual battle known as—well, that cannot be said. Perhaps, when necessary, one could refer to it as "The Affair" or "The Battle" or "The Clash." That is because this passage follows the tradition deployed across Ohio State's ca—uhh—province of knowledge-spreading. During the week of the encounter between the bitter rivals, that pesky thirteenth letter is crossed out with red tape on every sign in the area. Any utterance of the banned letter will trigger scornful looks. Enough violations of the weeklong rule can earn one a suggested relocation to the adversary's territory.

Okay, it's time to reinstate the letter "M" into this entry. Certainly, the Mathematics Tower on W. 18th Ave. receives a hefty dose of red tape. So does the McPherson Laboratory for the Department of Astronomy down the street. The Bill and Mae McCorkle Aquatic Pavilion gets a bit of a makeover, and even parking garages, with large cement rods overhead that state a maximum clearance, merit an alteration. Mirror Lake loses its chief, capital letter for a week. Ohio Stadium is forced to drop the very end of its moniker.

The campus' historical marker detailing the career of legendary head coach Woody Hayes, for one week of the year, reads as follows:

"Over his 28-year coaching career, Woody Hayes (1913–1987) ce-ented The Ohio State University's tradition of football excellence while a-assing one of the -ost i-pressive records in college football. Wayne Woodrow Hayes grew up in Newco-erstown and graduated fro- Denison University in 1935; after coaching two years at Denison and three at -ia-i, he began coaching at Ohio State in 1951. He led the Buckeyes to 205 wins, thirteen Big Ten titles, and five national cha-pionships. Passionate and co--itted to victory, Hayes fielded highly disciplined tea-s, characterized by his trade-ark "three yards and a cloud of dust" running offense and staunch defense. Off the field, he stressed acade-ic achieve-ent and taught history during the offseason."

All in all, the entire campus receives a facelift of sorts. Some "M's" can be harder to find and subsequently remove than others. The letter is an essential part of the alphabet. But in Columbus, it is unwelcome each year in late November.

. . . .

Relive the Top 10 Ohio State–Michigan Games

It seems as though every November, something is on the line when Ohio State and Michigan go to war. Often, the Big Ten regular season championship hangs in the balance. In the past, a Rose Bowl berth typically awaited the winner. With so much at stake on an annual basis, there have been an overwhelming number of unforgettable games recorded by the two rivals. Here is a breakdown of the top 10 games in the history of the rivalry.

No. 10: The Shootout
2013: Ohio State 42, Michigan 41

Boom. There it was.

Defensive back Tyvis Powell could not believe it. Sometimes the most unexpected events are the ones everyone expects to happen.

Few anticipated Michigan would come within a successful two-point conversion of an upset win against No. 3 Ohio State. The Buckeyes' defense, however, was ready for the Wolverines' attempt at a knockout in the 2013 edition of "The Game."

In an affair that packed more punch than anyone could have envisioned, a spectacle that showcased the perennial distaste between two rivals, a gut-wrenching production filled with swings of emotion and dripping with unscripted drama, Ohio State escaped. It survived. It advanced, its 12–0 record unblemished, 24-game win streak, and contention for a ticket to the BCS Championship Game intact.

It was a unanimous decision, but—for 59 minutes and 28 seconds—it was a highly contested one. There was no TKO, despite the hooks landed amid a second-quarter skirmish that resulted in three ejections and no love lost between schools that had been playing for more than a century.

Ohio State eked out a 42–41 win at Michigan Stadium on November 30, 2013, a victory preserved in the waning moments by Powell's pick of a pass by Wolverines quarterback Devin Gardner.

"He threw the ball," Powell said, "I ran out, listened to coach [Kerry] Coombs and boom, there it was."

It could have been anybody. Safety C.J. Barnett had talked about it all week. He was going to be the one to make a defining play, one that ended up on highlight reels or in an HBO documentary that details numerous examples of the schools foiling each other's national title hopes.

It was not Barnett, though. Powell made the play. And after the game, he had a message for his defensive backfield companion.

"Yeah, I"m going to be on the HBO series," he told Barnett.

Gardner had connected with receiver Devin Funchess for a two-yard touchdown to set up the decisive conversion attempt, as Michigan coach Brady Hoke opted to stow his special teams unit on the sideline.

"I would have done the same thing," said Ohio State coach Urban Meyer. "You go win the game there. No question."

Running back Carlos Hyde explained Michigan's decision-making with his own reasoning.

"They didn't want to go to overtime," Hyde said. "They knew what would've happened, so they tried to go for two and that didn't work out."

Meyer called a timeout to provide his defense with a momentary reprieve. As Powell prepared to return to the line of scrimmage, Coombs shouted some final advice in his direction. He told the Bedford, Ohio, native to keep an eye out for a receiver to motion

Ohio State defeated Michigan for seven straight years, beginning in 2000.

DUKING IT OUT

The image of Marcus Hall, middle fingers extended high in the air above his 6'5" frame, lives on in the form of T-shirt art and Internet memes. The moment—one for which the Buckeyes' right guard apologized—proved to be merely a subplot in an unforgettable installment of the Ohio State–Michigan rivalry.

In the second quarter of Ohio State's 42–41 victory, three players were ejected after a skirmish fit with punches, shoves, and competitive juices often reserved for rivalry games. Freshman halfback Dontre Wilson returned a kickoff, became entangled with Michigan running back Dennis Norfleet, and suddenly found himself surrounded by a circle of blue-clad Wolverines players. Once Wilson's teammates intervened to rescue the speedster, all hell broke loose. Wilson threw a punch. Quarterback Braxton Miller rushed in from the sideline and tugged at the face mask of Michigan defensive back Dymonte Thomas. Ohio State's offensive linemen followed Miller onto the field.

"I saw Braxton run out there," said center Corey Linsley, "and I was like, 'Man, I need to go get that guy.'"

Hall, Wilson, and Michigan linebacker Royce Jenkins-Stone were all tossed from the game. Hall slammed his helmet to the ground, kicked

to the right and form a set of three targets before running an angle route. Powell recognized the play from his film study and from practice. So he swapped assignments with linebacker Josh Perry, who pressured the quarterback. Gardner dropped back and swiftly fired the football into Powell's paws.

"I was thinking to myself, 'Coach Coombs is a genius,'" said Powell, who could not keep a smile from creeping across his face following Ohio State's win.

the team bench, stomped his feet, and flared his middle fingers to the crowd en route to the locker room. He subsequently sat out the following week's affair, the Big Ten Championship Game against Michigan State. Hall's sideline tirade earned the Ohio State coaching staff a public reprimand from the Big Ten, "for failing in its duty to effectively manage the process of escorting an ejected student-athlete from the playing field to the locker room."

"We shouldn't be out there doing that," running back Carlos Hyde said after the game. "We haven't done that all year. Even though this is a big rivalry game, that's not our game. We had to refocus and get back to doing what we do best."

This was not the first example of horseplay between the two schools. Bad blood existed long before Hall flipped the bird to those among the 113,511 in attendance at the Big House who were wearing blue. Ohio State receiver David Boston and Michigan cornerback Charles Woodson did as much talking with their arms and hands as they did with their incessant jawing at each other in 1997. Michigan running back Michael Shaw received an onslaught of uncivil remarks from Buckeyes players and fans when he slammed his shoulder into Ohio State's Grant Schwartz in the tunnel at The Horseshoe an hour before kickoff in 2009.

"You don't want anybody to fight," said linebacker Ryan Shazier, "but there are a lot of emotions going on both sides and a lot of guys are really hyped and things just happen. It's not acceptable, but I am not surprised that it happened."

It could have been anyone making the season-defining play, one reminiscent of Will Allen's interception of John Navarre in 2002, a game-ending pick that permitted Fiesta Bowl promoters to print Ohio State's ticket to the national title game. Who would have pegged Powell as the protagonist in this contest?

In a back-and-forth offensive shootout—the teams combined for 1,129 total yards—Powell's opportunism on defense paved the way for the Buckeyes to prevail. As soon as he snagged the errant pass, he dropped to the ground and tucked away what he called "the most prized possession."

"That was our season on the line," Powell said, interrupted by an unrelenting giggle. "12–0. The gold pants. Chances for the national championship. It just hit me, like, 'Wow, I kind of saved the season.'"

It required some wishing and hoping. Ohio State quarterback Braxton Miller said he prayed before Michigan's two-point conversion attempt. Backup quarterback Kenny Guiton told Powell he prayed "like, 80 times."

"That was an instant classic," Meyer said.

Boom. That, it was.

No. 9: The Pick
2002: Ohio State 14, Michigan 9

One second. It is enough time for a team to run a play, enough time to keep a defense on its heels and a crowd on the edge of its seat. It is what remained on the clock after Michigan quarterback John Navarre slung a pass a few yards beyond the back of the end zone. There was no home-field advantage from the clock operator at Ohio Stadium. The Wolverines were granted one last chance to sack Ohio State's national title aspirations.

Twenty-four yards. It is enough ground to cover that Ohio State sent three defensive backs inside the 10-yard line at the start of the play. Navarre would not be able to find his tailback open in the flat, able to squirm free for a touchdown. He had to throw deep, to the end zone. A 23-yard gain would not cut it. The Buckeyes rushed three down linemen and manned Michigan's four wideouts and one tailback with eight defenders.

One play. Trailing 14–9, Michigan had driven into Ohio State territory, but with about two minutes left, Buckeyes defensive end Will Smith recovered a Navarre fumble at the 35-yard line. The game's first turnover offered Ohio State an opportunity to run out the clock, but the Buckeyes went three-and-out and punted the ball back to Michigan with one minute remaining. The Wolverines converted a fourth-and-10 and then three more first downs—one on a pass interference violation by cornerback Chris Gamble—all of which stopped the clock. Navarre's overthrow set up the final snap.

Thirty-four years. Ohio State's previous outright national championship had come in 1968. That was a Woody Hayes team made up of sophomores oozing with talent. The Buckeyes, with 11 All-Americans and six first-round NFL draft picks, steamrolled their opponents en route to a 10–0 mark. They walloped the Wolverines 50–14 to advance to the Rose Bowl, in which they topped USC 27–16 to claim the national title. After more than three decades, the Buckeyes had another shot at a title game and only Michigan stood in their way. This team, though, eked its way through its schedule. Ohio State entered its Saturday matinee with Michigan having won five of its previous nine games by seven points or fewer. One more high-strung, tension-filled afternoon beneath Columbus' gray skies separated Ohio State from another shot at national glory.

Three steps. Navarre, back a few yards in a shotgun formation, took the snap from center. He shuffled backward three steps and twisted his upper body to the left. He had his sights fixated on sophomore receiver Braylon Edwards from the get-go. His offensive line provided plenty of protection and he uncorked a pass from about the 32-yard line.

Three defenders. There was Mike Doss, a three-time All-Big Ten and All-American selection and the conference's Defensive Player of the Year. As soon as Doss realized where Navarre planned to deliver the football, he left his designated area of the field and made a beeline for Edwards. There was Chris Gamble, a two-way player (three ways if including special teams) and All-Big Ten selection. He spent the afternoon chasing Edwards around the field. He appeared to be in stride, step for step with Edwards until the receiver redirected his route and cut toward the middle of the field. Then there was

Will Allen, a defensive back who played in nickel packages. When Edwards squirmed free from Gamble, it left Allen to patrol the area. Gamble and Doss eventually collided with each other at the goal line, but not before Allen stepped in front of Edwards and snagged Navarre's pass at the 2-yard line. He stumbled forward, his right knee and then shoulder plunging into the grass. He curled up in a ball, protecting the football, and then bounced to his feet as fellow defensive back Donnie Nickey sprinted over to embrace him. The Buckeyes spilled out onto the field. Allen's game-ending pick sent Ohio State to the national title game.

Nickey jumped on Allen's back. Allen refused to let go of the football. Defensive lineman Simon Fraser joined the fray, as he pounced on Allen and knocked his teammate to the ground. The rest of the team followed suit.

On the national broadcast, play-by-play announcer Brent Musberger shouted: "Let's party, Columbus! Their 29th Big Ten Championship, and it is huge, as Maurice Clarett, Jim Tressel, and the Buckeyes will head to Arizona, where they will play for all of the Tostitos in the Fiesta Bowl on January 3."

"To win the big games," said linebacker Matt Wilhelm, "the home game against Michigan, to top off your career in the Ohio Stadium and have an opportunity to play in [the championship game] is something you dream about."

No. 8: Earle's Goodbye
1987: Ohio State 23, Michigan 20

Five days before Ohio State and Michigan squared off in the regular-season finale, university president Edward Jennings summoned athletic director Rick Bay to his office. It was then, around lunchtime on Monday, when Jennings informed Bay that head coach Earle Bruce would be fired after Saturday's affair with Michigan. Jennings swore Bay to secrecy, but Bay replied by saying: "If he goes, I go."

Word got out. By 4 o'clock that afternoon, the news of Bruce's impending pink slip spread throughout the state of Ohio. Fans showed up to Bruce's home in Worthington, a short drive from campus. Band members blared their instruments. Others chanted. Bruce stepped outside to greet the mob and he broke down and cried. He stressed that everyone focus on beating Michigan that week and not his job status.

"It really shook him," said Ohio State football historian Jack Park.

As the Buckeyes took the field at Michigan Stadium to warm up for the game, they sported white headbands with the name "Earle" on them.

"He didn't know anything about that," Park said. "That really touched his heart that they would do that."

Ohio State entered the meeting on a three-game skid. The three defeats came by a total of 10 points. Michigan had won three straight, but neither team arrived at the annual encounter with a national ranking. The Wolverines claimed a 13–0 lead in the second quarter. The Buckeyes narrowed the deficit to 13–7 at halftime, and on the first play after intermission, quarterback Tom Tupa connected on a short pass to freshman tailback Carlos Snow, who dashed 70 yards to the end zone.

"He just threw it out there, and there I was, all alone," Snow said.

Tupa later scored on a one-yard rush, but kicker Matt Frantz, who had been automatic on extra points, botched the kick, keeping Ohio State's lead at 20–13.

There was no overtime in 1987. The Buckeyes had already tied with LSU in Baton Rouge, Louisiana, in late September. Another tie would leave Bruce with a 5–5–2 season in his swan song. After Michigan knotted the game at 20–20, Ohio State moved the ball into Wolverines territory and faced a fourth-and-1 on the 10-yard line.

Frantz was standing side by side with his head coach. Bruce looked at the kicker. Frantz suggested they attempt the field goal, saying "Let's kick it." Bruce replied: "OK. Kick it in." Frantz converted the field goal with a little more than five minutes remaining. He raised both arms in the air in celebration as place holder Scott Powell jumped up and down on his way back to the sideline. The Buckeyes' defense held tight to seal the victory and allow Bruce to go out on top.

"It was very fitting," Park said.

Frantz said he talked to Jennings—not the most popular man on campus—before the contest and the school president told the kicker to instruct everyone on Ohio State's defense to think of his face if that tactic would motivate the team to dispatch its rival.

"Ohio State really wanted to win that one for Earle," Park said.

Bruce said there was "no sweeter victory in the world than a win over Michigan in your last game at Ohio State," especially after trailing by 13 in the first half. After Michigan quarterback Demetrius Brown heaved an incompletion 60 yards downfield from his goal line, Ohio State players joined efforts to carry Bruce, who donned a sports coat, tie, and fedora, off the field.

"That was satisfaction, seeing how happy he was," said linebacker Chris Spielman. "We can all look in the mirror and walk out of here proud. For a man to go through what he went through this week, to hold his composure, is the sign of a true man, a true Buckeye. He may not have all the charisma. He may not have all the personality. But there is no better football coach in America."

No. 7: Slipping Away
1996: Michigan 13, Ohio State 9

Ohio State's 31–23 loss to Michigan in 1995 left head coach John Cooper in a state of disarray

"I don't know if I've ever been this disappointed in my life," Cooper said after the Wolverines sprung a 31–23 upset on the previously unbeaten Buckeyes.

Just how talented was the 1995 team?

"Oh my goodness," said running back Eddie George, who won the Heisman Trophy that year. "We were young. We had some young players that weren't even starting that were future All-Americans, first-round players. There's no telling."

On the first play from scrimmage in the second half, Ohio State quarterback Bobby Hoying lofted a pass to the left sideline for receiver Terry Glenn, but Michigan's true freshman cornerback Charles Woodson intervened and picked it off. Cooper called it the turning point of the contest. Hoying was supposed to target his tight end in the middle of the field. Michigan converted the turnover into a touchdown, which extended the Wolverines' lead to 17–9.

"I saw that play and I said, 'Oh my. This is not going to be good,'" said Ohio State football historian Jack Park. "They kept getting stronger as that second half wore on."

Tshimanga Biakabutuka—say that name five times fast—rushed 37 times for 313 yards.

"You shouldn't be able to do that against any defense, especially the defense of the No. 2-ranked team in the country," said Michigan guard Joe Marinaro.

Michigan spread out its offensive line, in a version of the old split-T formation, which first became popular about 40 years earlier. Longtime Ohio State coach Woody Hayes even went down to the University of Oklahoma to spend time with the Sooners' head coach, Bud Wilkinson, who had implemented the scheme into his offense. The formation provides the rusher with more potential running lanes, though it also leaves the offense susceptible to defensive pressure because of the large gaps along the line. Biakabutuka said after the game that any of the reporters asking him questions could have run through the holes his offensive line had created.

"I've been playing football for six years, including high school, and I've never seen holes like that," he said.

At the start of the week, Biakabutuka had gone to Michigan head coach Lloyd Carr and told him he planned to outplay George, despite the Buckeye's reputation as an elite player.

"That's the thing that legends are made of," Park said. "And he really did."

The Buckeyes' Rose Bowl dreams were dashed. Their No. 2 ranking was slashed. They settled for a Citrus Bowl date with Tennessee. The Volunteers prevailed 20–14.

Well, Ohio State entered its annual affair against Michigan with another unblemished record a year later. Could Cooper's crew get revenge, or would it suffer a second straight punishing blow at the hands of its nemesis up north?

It was eerie, almost. Brian Griese took over at quarterback in the second half for the Wolverines, who trailed 9–0 at intermission. Keith Jackson, on the national broadcast, said: "Griese was at the throttle a year ago when Biakabutuka had the big game and Michigan spoiled Ohio State's dreams of an undefeated season."

Jackson then shifted his focus to the play at hand. Michigan broke the huddle, with the ball just outside of the 31-yard line. Nearly a minute had elapsed off the clock in the second half when Griese took the snap, shifted three steps back, and fired a quick pass to receiver Tai Streets, who hauled in the football at the 39-yard line, turned upfield, and darted toward the end zone.

"I think the Ohio State team was almost defeated when Streets went the distance there," Park said.

Cornerback Shawn Springs had slipped. By the time he and linebacker Andy Katzenmoyer gave chase, Streets was gone. Michigan had its first score, and what proved to be the game's only touchdown.

"All of a sudden, they came to life," Cooper said.

Michigan tacked on a pair of field goals and Ohio State's offense remained stuck in neutral. The Wolverines emerged with a 13–9 victory, and for the second consecutive season, Lloyd Carr's bunch ruined the Buckeyes' attempt at a perfect season.

"It's a disappointment and almost a failure," said senior linebacker Greg Bellisari.

Park was sitting in the south end of Ohio Stadium in 1996. Memories of that contest have yet to fade. He shakes his head at the thought of the Buckeyes failing to capitalize on three first-half possessions that resulted in field goals instead of touchdowns. And, of course, he cannot forget Streets streaking down the middle of the field.

"I can see that guy running yet," Park said. "For most people, we thought, 'We're probably not going to win this game.'"

Ohio State produced two of the more disheartening defeats in program history in back-to-back years.

"If I had to pick one of the two that were more disappointing, I would probably say the 1996 game," Park said. "But it would be really close."

No. 6: The Comeback
1975: Ohio State 21, Michigan 14

Michigan had not lost at home in more than six years, an unbeaten string of 41 consecutive games at the Big House. In the Wolverines' previous three games at home, they had outscored the opposition 152–7. Ohio State running back Archie Griffin had amassed more yards on the ground than any rusher in NCAA history and had rattled off 31 consecutive games of at least 100 yards.

Both streaks ended on a chilly, windy afternoon in Ann Arbor. With about seven minutes left, Michigan scored a touchdown on fourth-and-goal from the 1-yard line. The Wolverines held a 14–7 advantage. With three minutes left, Ohio State fullback Pete Johnson plunged into the end zone on fourth-and-goal from the 1 to even the score. Three plays later, Michigan quarterback Rick Leach heaved an interception, secured by Ohio State's Ray Griffin, who returned the pick to the Michigan 3-yard line. On the ensuing snap, Johnson rumbled into the end zone and Ohio State had itself a seven-point lead that it would not relinquish.

"They outplayed us in the first half and the third quarter," said Ohio State head coach Woody Hayes. "Then wasn't it amazing how the game changed."

Woody called the fourth-quarter spurt "the greatest comeback I've ever had as coach."

The 11–0 Buckeyes advanced to the Rose Bowl, which they lost 23–10 to UCLA, a team they had dispatched three months earlier in Los Angeles. Still, the 1975 victory over Michigan marked the fourth consecutive meeting between the rivals without an Ohio State defeat. And the Buckeyes notched a victory despite only 46 yards rushing on 19 carries for Griffin.

"If you know Arch," Woody said, "he'll trade all his records for a victory, like this one."

No. 5: The Goal-Line Stand
1972: Ohio State 14, Michigan 11

Bo Schembechler was not going to settle for a tie. His Michigan team was either going to prevail and proceed to Pasadena, California, or the Wolverines would go down in a blaze of scarlet and gray glory. In its bid to spoil Michigan's perfect season, Ohio State halted its rival at the goal line to seal a 14–11 victory at The Horseshoe.

Trailing by three midway through the fourth quarter, Michigan moved the ball to the Ohio State 5-yard line. Three consecutive plunges forward inched the ball to within a foot of the end zone. The

Wolverines had fourth down, with the game hanging in the balance. A field goal would have secured a tie.

"I never considered it," Schembechler said. "I didn't want a tie. We wanted to win."

Quarterback Dennis Franklin tried to sneak the football across the goal line himself, but he was stuffed by the middle of Ohio State's defensive line. With seven seconds remaining in the first half, Franklin fumbled the transfer of the snap from the Ohio State 1-yard line. The Buckeyes eventually punted it back to Michigan in the fourth quarter, but the Wolverines never threatened to score the rest of the way.

After Michigan turned the ball over in the closing seconds, thousands of fans spilled out onto the field to celebrate. They tore down the goal post in the south end zone. The game was not quite over, however. Ohio State coaches ran out onto the field to shoo the fans back into the stands. Quarterback Greg Hare eventually kneeled down to run out the final few seconds.

No. 4: The Snow Bowl
1950: Michigan 9, Ohio State 3

Ohio State's Wes Fesler, in his last hurrah as Buckeyes head coach, did not want to play the game. He deemed the conditions too treacherous. Fritz Crisler, Michigan's athletic director who had served as head coach from 1938 to 1947, thought otherwise. He said if Ohio State opted to cancel the November 25, 1950, encounter between the two schools—the home team had the final say on the matter—then the game would never be played. Michigan had no plans to make a separate trek to Columbus.

Ohio State eventually conceded and signed off on the two teams squaring off in a winter wonderland at Ohio Stadium. Athletic director Dick Larkins did not want to deal with refunding the tickets used by the 50,000 who braved the blizzard and attended the contest.

Had the game not been played, Ohio State would have been awarded the Big Ten title. With a win, Michigan would capture the conference crown and a trip to the Rose Bowl in Pasadena, California.

"It should have never been played," said Ohio State football historian Jack Park.

Unrelenting snow tumbled from the sky, with gusting winds spraying it all over and inhibiting the vision of everyone at the stadium. The conditions grew worse as the afternoon unfolded. The temperature hovered around 10 degrees. Michigan's kicker said that when he dropped back to punt, he could not even see Ohio State's punt returner. The swirling snow created a wet football, which resulted in 10 total fumbles between the two teams.

Ohio State's Vic Janowicz, the Heisman Trophy winner that year and a player who did everything for the Buckeyes, including kick, converted a 28-yard field goal through the whiteout to provide Fesler's bunch with a 3–0 advantage in the first quarter. That proved to be the only offense-induced scoring in the game. Volunteers stood at the back of the end zone, ready to wield their brooms and sweep away the snow so everyone could see the goal lines and the sideline yard-markers. At least, until the fluffy white stuff swiftly recovered the barren areas. Janowicz said the game was "a nightmare," adding that his hands were numb and he was not sure how he hung onto the ball.

Michigan first scored on a safety, the result of a blocked kick that bounced out of the end zone. With less than a minute remaining in the first half, Michigan's Tony Momsen swatted away a punt and pounced on the football in the end zone for a touchdown. Michigan completed the 9–3 victory despite zero first downs in the game.

Ohio State completed 3 of 18 pass attempts for 25 yards, with two interceptions. The Buckeyes rushed 40 times for 16 yards. In total, Ohio State gained 41 yards on 58 plays, an average of 0.7 yards per play. The Buckeyes punted the ball away on 21 occasions. In fact, the teams often called for a punt on first or second down, feeling they had a better chance at scoring or causing havoc with the other team in possession.

The Wolverines attempted nine passes, but did not complete any of them. They gained only 27 yards on 37 rushes. All told, they averaged a little more than half of a yard per play on 46 snaps. They punted the ball away 24 times. And they emerged victorious.

No. 3: The Streak Snapper
1969: Michigan 24, Ohio State 12

After Woody Hayes' coaching days ran out, there was a dinner held to honor the man who racked up 205 wins and 13 conference championships. He stood at the podium, and, while discussing his team's 1969 loss to Michigan, he looked down at longtime Wolverines coach Bo Schembechler, who was in the audience, and said: "God damn you. You will never win a bigger game than that."

"He was right," Schembechler recalled, years later. "I don't think I ever did."

Rewind to 1968. Ohio State conquered college football. On the backs of the "Super Sophomores," the Buckeyes rattled off 10 consecutive victories en route to a perfect season, capped with a Rose Bowl win against USC, which clinched Ohio State the national championship. In the final regular-season game, the Buckeyes demolished No. 4 Michigan, 50-14.

Woody referred to it as the "best victory we ever had," as he lauded how players on both sides of the ball performed.

"The offense would have a good day and the defense would stutter around some," Woody said. "Then, another game, it would be the other way around. We said that if they ever put it together [and] both played well the same day, we would have something. This is it."

The final score, though, only tells part of the story. Late in the contest, the Buckeyes gripped a commanding 44–14 lead and possessed the ball on Michigan's 1-yard line. It was first-and-goal and Woody deployed the backups on offense. Bill Long was in at quarterback. He handed to Ray Huff, who lost a yard as he was stuffed trying to run up the middle. Jim Otis, the team's starting tailback, had already tallied three rushing touchdowns on the afternoon. He was convinced he could notch a fourth, so Woody re-inserted him into the huddle. Otis found an opening on the left side of the line and plunged into the end zone before tossing the football into the stands in celebration.

Instead of kicking the extra point, the Buckeyes went for two. Legend has it that, when asked why he went for two, Woody replied: "Because I couldn't go for three." That quote will forever be linked to the surly coach. Long contends that Woody would never actually attempt to run up the score. He knew better than to hand his opponents—especially his archrival—extra means of motivation. Long served as the holder on kicks. The team's long snapper, however, was injured, so Long turned to the sideline to ask Woody what to do. Woody waved him back into the huddle. So Long called a passing play, but he threw incomplete.

Nevertheless, Woody's quote fueled the Wolverines, who sought vengeance the following season under Schembechler, the first-year coach. They applied masking tape—decorated with the number "50" on it—to their helmets during practice all week leading up to the rematch so they were forced to remember the number of points Ohio State had amassed the year before. Ohio State football historian Jack Park said there is no question that "the two-point conversion had an impact on them."

"That became the biggest thing," Long said. "They had it on their boards about going for two and Woody's quote. They were the only team to beat us in '69."

The Buckeyes entered the 1969 Michigan game winners of 22 straight contests. In 1968, when they completed an undefeated season, they had some close calls along the way. In 1969, they spent the duration of their season ranked No. 1 in the nation. Their "closest" calls prior to the Michigan game were a pair of 27-point road wins. Then, the Buckeyes ventured to Ann Arbor, Michigan, on a brisk, sobering Saturday afternoon.

Rex Kern tossed interceptions on each of Ohio State's final two drives of the first half. He threw two more picks in the second half before he was relieved by Ron Maciejowski, who accounted for three turnovers himself. Altogether, Ohio State turned it over seven times and the Buckeyes proved unable to claw back from a 24–12 deficit.

"The thing that had the most impact on that game was the leadership of Bo Schembechler," Park said. "He told those guys in the spring that Woody Hayes was going to bring his team in there on November 22 and they would be undefeated and they would be the No. 1 team in the country. 'Rest assured, that is going to happen. We can beat them if you'll start thinking about this right now and get ready for it. We can beat these guys.'

"Their whole season was planned to beat Ohio State. And he was right. Ohio State had never been behind that season. They had never been tested.

"It's a great, great example of what leadership at the top of an organization can do for that organization."

Michigan earned a trip to the Rose Bowl—they would have regardless of the outcome, since the Big Ten had a no-repeat rule in effect at the time—where they fell short against USC by a 10–3 score. Michigan snapped Ohio State's program record-long win streak. In his 10th game as Wolverines coach, Schembechler had the signature victory of a lifetime.

"That is the most significant football game in the Big Ten, ever," Park said. "It is the biggest win in Michigan history and I think it is the most devastating loss in Ohio State history."

No. 2: The Tie
1973: Ohio State 10, Michigan 10

Bo Schembechler called it "the greatest disappointment" of his coaching career. And his team did not even lose the game.

Michigan and Ohio State both entered their 1973 clash with unblemished records. The Buckeyes (9–0) were ranked No. 1 in the nation. The Wolverines (10–0) checked in at No. 4. On a gloomy day in Ann Arbor, before a then-NCAA record crowd of 105,233, both teams relied on their running games in hopes of clinching a Big Ten title, a Rose Bowl berth, and a potential national championship. Ohio State, behind Archie Griffin's 99 yards on the ground, held a 10–0 lead at halftime. The Wolverines evened the score with a fourth-quarter touchdown, but Michigan kicker Mike Lantry missed a pair of lengthy boots in the waning minutes and quarterback Dennis Franklin left the contest with a broken collarbone. Ohio State attempted three passes on its final drive, but all three fell incomplete. Buckeyes quarterback Greg Hare went 0-for-4 on the afternoon. The game ended in a 10–10 deadlock.

Michigan thought it would still receive the Rose Bowl nod.

"Everybody, including Woody Hayes, congratulated me after the game and said, 'Oh, you'll do a great job in the Rose Bowl,'" Schembechler said.

Though the Big Ten had abandoned its no-repeat mandate, Ohio State had played in Pasadena the previous year. The decision was determined by a vote on a conference call among the league's athletic directors. A day after the 10–10 tie, Ohio State was selected to participate in the Rose Bowl. Schembechler was livid.

"If you look at the game, we outplayed [Ohio State]," Schembechler said. "If you look at tradition, Ohio State had played in the Rose Bowl the year before. So everything indicated that we were going to go to the Rose Bowl. It was strictly a political thing. And I assume the fact that our great quarterback, Dennis Franklin, broke his collarbone in the fourth quarter of that game on a blitz, that they might have used that as an excuse."

Ohio State knocked off USC in the Rose Bowl 42–21. Michigan's season ended with the tie.

"That whole thing upset me to no end," Schembechler said.

No. 1: The Game of the Century
2006: Ohio State 42, Michigan 39

Rarely does a game with an overwhelming buildup exceed the hype. For the first time in the history of the rivalry—this was the 103rd encounter—Ohio State and Michigan entered their annual meeting as the No. 1 and No. 2 ranked teams in the nation. For the first time in 31 years, the adversaries arrived at the affair with unblemished records. For those reasons, the 2006 matchup was dubbed "The Game of the Century." The game ultimately drew a 13.0 TV rating, becoming the most watched regular-season college football game in 13 years.

Buckeyes quarterback Troy Smith entered the contest as the Heisman Trophy favorite. Michigan entered the game with the third-ranked defense in the country and the top-ranked rushing defense. Ohio State had spent the entire season as the No. 1 team in the polls and in the BCS rankings. The Buckeyes demolished their first 11 opponents by an average of 28 points per game, and only once—at Illinois—did Jim Tressel's bunch win by fewer than 17 points. In early September, Ohio State knocked off then-No. 2 Texas in Austin by a 24–7 score. Michigan played its previous opponents a bit closer, but the Wolverines steadily ascended up the polls as the season progressed. Lloyd Carr's squad throttled Notre Dame, ranked No. 2 at the time, on the road, 47–21, in mid-September.

As the week unfolded, the hype gained momentum.

BEATING "MICHIGAN"

At the age of 11, Grant Reed made it his mission to beat Michigan. Reed, who lived about an hour outside of Columbus, loved the Buckeyes. He was sick of discussing his brain tumor, though, so doctors asked him to call the cancer by a different name. Reed chose "Michigan." Not that he needed more motivation to overcome the unforgiving disease, but now Reed could discuss a goal shared—on a different level, for sure—by any Ohio State backer. He wanted to defeat Michigan.

In May 2012, Reed underwent a 16½-hour surgery to remove a brain tumor, but he could not move his left side or speak or see properly. He spent almost 10 weeks at the hospital and received radiation, chemotherapy, and occupational and speech therapies. On Saturdays when Reed was stuck at the hospital, his family joined him and together they watched Ohio State's games. Head coach Urban Meyer visited him at Nationwide Children's Hospital in Columbus that December.

Reed's parents were members of the Ohio State Marching Band. They got engaged at halftime of a game against Michigan.

Fourteen months after the initial surgery, Reed's prognosis indicated that he had, in fact, beaten cancer. Michigan coach Brady Hoke was just fine with that.

"We were glad," Hoke said. "We were excited for that young man. And being a father, our children are so important and you try and put yourself through what that family has gone through. So him beating Michigan, in this context, we were all for it."

Hoke offered Reed's family four tickets to the 2013 edition of the Ohio State–Michigan game. The family ventured to Ann Arbor, Michigan, and watched the Buckeyes do what the boy had done: beat Michigan.

"I really don't think that anything needs to be said," Michigan offensive tackle Jake Long said. "Everybody knows the goals we set and what's at stake in this game."

The game was set for 3:30 PM ET, rather than the traditional noon kickoff. ESPN's College GameDay set up shop on Ohio State's campus.

"I think this is about as big as it gets," former Michigan coach Bo Schembechler said the week of the game. "I don't know what else you can do. Two teams that have been dominant all year long. I don't care who it is. There's no rivalry that compares with this. This is the greatest college football rivalry there is. I don't see that changing."

Talk had already commenced about the teams meeting a second time in the BCS Championship Game, so long as the outcome of the regular season meeting proved close. Debate grew about whether an outside team deserved a shot at the winner, or whether, no matter the result, Ohio State and Michigan were, in fact, the two best teams in the country.

"Once you beat a team, it's over," Schembechler said. "If you're a loser, of course you want to play those guys again. But I would not be in favor of that under any circumstances."

Four days after he supplied that sentiment and one day after he gave the Wolverines his annual pep talk, Schembechler collapsed and died, a result of a battle with heart disease. The man who racked up 194 wins and 13 Big Ten titles at Michigan passed away the day before perhaps the most significant game in the history of the Ohio State–Michigan rivalry.

Prior to kickoff, the Ohio Stadium scoreboard displayed a video tribute to Schembechler. The PA announcer read: "Michigan has lost a coach and patriarch. The Big Ten has lost a legend and icon. Ohio State has lost an alumnus and friend."

Michigan running back Mike Hart scored a touchdown on the Wolverines' opening possession. That marked the final time

Michigan held the lead that afternoon. The Buckeyes immediately answered, as Smith connected with receiver Roy Hall to tie the game 7–7. In the second quarter, Ohio State reached the end zone three times. Freshman running back Chris "Beanie" Wells scored on a 52-yard scamper, receiver Ted Ginn Jr. hauled in a 39-yard touchdown and, after Michigan closed to within 21–14, receiver Anthony Gonzalez snagged an eight-yard touchdown reception with 20 seconds remaining in the half. The Buckeyes carried a 14-point lead into intermission.

The Wolverines scored 10 unanswered points to begin the third quarter, as they narrowed their deficit to 28–24, but Ohio State running back Antonio Pittman dashed 56 yards to the end zone to quell Michigan's momentum. Hart plunged in from one yard out to make it a 35–31 game, but Smith fired a 13-yard touchdown pass to receiver Brian Robiskie for a 42–31 lead with about five minutes left on the clock.

Chad Henne tossed a touchdown and two-point conversion with a little over two minutes left, but Ginn Jr. recovered Michigan's onside kick attempt and the Buckeyes ran out the clock to clinch a spot in the national title game. The teams combined for 900 yards of offense. Smith totaled 316 yards through the air and four touchdowns, which propelled him to win the Heisman Trophy.

The crowd spilled out onto the field after the final whistle. Ohio Stadium became a sea of scarlet. Offensive tackle Kirk Barton arrived at the postgame interview room with what he said was a $125 cigar in his mouth. He said he also purchased a $350 bottle of Dom Perignon to celebrate the victory.

There was no rematch in Glendale, Arizona. The teams remained Nos. 1 and 2 in the BCS standings for another week, but USC jumped Michigan with a win over Notre Dame and, after USC lost to UCLA and Florida topped Arkansas in the SEC Championship Game, the Gators ultimately merited the No. 2 ranking.

About a half hour after the conclusion of Ohio State's 42–39 win against Michigan, the Ohio Lottery Pick 4 game revealed a winning combination of 4-2-3-9, which had a 10,000 to 1 chance of happening. A lottery spokeswoman said 401 $1 bets were placed for that numerical sequence. Each bet earned $5,000.

· ·

Proudly Sing "We Don't Give a Damn"

O hio State's long-standing traditions include a litany of prideful tunes. One of them cuts straight to the chase. There is no guessing the meaning of the lyrics or reading between the lines. It is as straightforward as it gets.

"We don't give a damn for the whole state of Michigan"

At any point during a sporting event, at a bar on campus, or really at any establishment in the state of Ohio, alumni or Buckeyes backers might break out into song.

"The whole state of Michigan, the whole state of Michigan"

The words are candid and easy to memorize. The motive is obvious. Thus, anyone with ties to Ohio State can instantly recognize the tune and join in on the presentation.

"We don't give a damn for the whole state of Michigan"

The song dates back at least to 1942, when it made a cameo in the movie *The Male Animal*, a film starring Henry Fonda that was based on a Broadway play written two years prior by Ohio State alumni James Thurber and Elliott Nugent.

"We're from O-hi-o"

The movie takes place on the weekend of an important football game between Midwestern University and its rival, the University of Michigan. Midwestern University is said to represent Ohio State in the movie.

"We're from O-hi-o...O-H-"

The movie premiered in March 1942 in Columbus, Ohio. Nugent directed the film.

"We're from O-hi-o...-I-O"

The Ohio State Marching Band shouts the song as it filters into St. John Arena for the Skull Session pep rally prior to every home football game.

"We don't give a damn for the whole state of Michigan"

"The whole state of Michigan, the whole state of Michigan"

"We don't give a damn for the whole state of Michigan"

"We're from O-hi-o"

· ·

Learn About the Ten Year War

In 1950, Woody Hayes led Miami University to a 9–1 record and a Salad Bowl victory against Arizona State in Phoenix. Bo Schembechler played tackle on that team. Woody parlayed that brilliant season in Oxford, Ohio, into the Ohio State head coaching job. Upon assuming that position, he asked Schembechler to join him as a graduate assistant.

Schembechler said he took "so many hours of graduate work," made the coffee for the coaches every morning, picked up prospects at the airport, and ran a ton of errands. Quite the glamorous gig. Schembechler completed a tour of duty with the U.S. Army and then served as a coach at Presbyterian, Bowling Green, and Northwestern—under head coach Ara Parseghian, who succeeded Woody at Miami after being his assistant coach for a year. In 1958, Woody recruited him back to Columbus, where he spent five years as an assistant coach.

"In spite of everything, I enjoyed it," Schembechler said. "We had many good teams and we had some bad teams. It was Ohio State football and it was good."

Of course, Woody and Bo butted heads on a regular basis.

"He was the worst guy in the world to work for," Schembechler said. "But I wouldn't change that experience for anything in the world. I learned a lot."

Deep down, the two appreciated and respected each other.

"He was a flawless guy personally," Schembechler said. "Good, honest Christian man. He was a good leader."

Schembechler ventured back to Miami University, where he became head coach of his alma mater in 1963. He spent six seasons in Oxford before taking over at Michigan. His first affair against his old mentor was the most memorable. Ohio State entered the final week of the 1969 regular season riding a 22-game winning streak and needing one more victory to secure its second straight national title. A Michigan Stadium crowd of 103,588—a record at the time— witnessed history, as the Wolverines upset the Buckeyes 24–12. Michigan players carried Schembechler off of the field. Woody returned to Columbus and immediately started prepping for the 1970 rivalry game.

Thus, the Ten Year War was born.

"It was our strategy here at Michigan to do something to beat Ohio State every day," Schembechler said, "and even if it's in the first meeting to talk about it. But we're going to do something every day."

During Woody's tenure, the Buckeyes practiced specifically for Michigan at least one day per week.

"If they were playing Indiana or Northwestern and those teams were really poor and Ohio State was undefeated," said Ohio State football historian Jack Park, "they may have worked on Michigan two or three days that week and not tell anybody, although I think it was pretty generally known that they were doing it. The Michigan game was everything to both of those guys. That's what they did. They did anything they could to try to get an advantage over the other one."

Over the ensuing decade, Michigan topped Ohio State five times. The Buckeyes captured four victories against the Wolverines. The teams tied in the 1973 affair, when both sides entered without a loss. Each year from 1969 to 1981, either Ohio State or Michigan represented the Big Ten in the Rose Bowl. During the Ten Year War, each side proceeded to Pasadena on five occasions. Eventually, the conference earned the nickname "Big Two, Little Eight." Both coaches prepared for their rival, at times, in lieu of planning for that week's actual opponent.

"The other Big Ten teams, frankly, could not measure up to these two," Schembechler said. "So they had an opportunity to work on other things."

Michigan 24, Ohio State 12
1969: The 1968 Buckeyes rolled through their schedule and completed an undefeated national championship season. And yet, many believe the 1969 squad was stronger.

"The '69 team may have been the strongest Ohio State football team ever fielded," Park said.

Paul Hornung of the *Columbus Dispatch* once suggested to Park that in 1969, Woody could have sent his second-stringers on the road almost any weekend and still beat just about any team in the country.

"They were so strong and so deep at every position," Park said. "Maybe there was a little bit of complacency. They were 17-point favorites going into the game."

Woody told Schembechler he would never capture a victory as impressive as the one he did against Ohio State in 1969. After the trek back to Columbus, he stormed into his office and started planning for the following season's rematch.

"I'm sure he was working on it by Sunday," Park said. "He may have started it Saturday night."

Ohio State 20, Michigan 9

1970: The following year, the Buckeyes sought and achieved redemption. Both teams entered the affair unbeaten, and the Buckeyes prevailed with a 20–9 win. They more than doubled Michigan in total yardage (329 to 155) and they secured the victory with 10 points in the fourth quarter.

Michigan 10, Ohio State 7

1971: Woody's bunch arrived in Ann Arbor, Michigan, with a 6–3 mark and without a national ranking. The Wolverines were undefeated at 10–0. Michigan scored a touchdown in the closing minutes to grab a 10–7 lead and Ohio State quarterback Don Lamka threw an interception to seal the loss for the Buckeyes, who argued that Michigan was guilty of interference on the turnover. Woody launched into a frustration-based tirade and the players engaged in a bench-clearing brawl.

Ohio State 14, Michigan 11

1972: For the second straight season, Michigan entered the meeting ranked No. 3 and boasting a 10–0 record. The Buckeyes stood at 8–1 and held the lead for most of the afternoon. Ohio State emerged victorious 14–11 thanks to a pair of goal-line stops.

Ohio State 10, Michigan 10

1973: The Buckeyes entered at 9–0, ranked No. 1 in the nation. The Wolverines entered at 10–0, ranked No. 4 in the nation. Ohio State could not pull out a victory in Ann Arbor, though. Then again, neither could Michigan. Wait, what? The Wolverines missed a field goal with 28 seconds left and, for the first time in nearly a quarter-century, the teams tied.

EXTRA POINTS

Just for Kicks

Woody Hayes and Bo Schembechler did anything in their power to secure an advantage over their adversary. One year, there was a new brand of shoe coming out that was said to combat the slick grass of a wet field on a rainy day. Supposedly, Schembechler had ordered the shoes and he was going to hand them out to his players. Woody got wind of the story and decided to snoop around to learn more about the shoes. If they would help to prevent his players from slipping or losing their balance, he wanted his players wearing them—especially if Michigan's players had access to them.

"I don't know if Bo planted that story or how he got it going, but there was no such shoe," said Ohio State football historian Jack Park. "There was no shoe at all. But Woody spent a lot of time trying to find out what that was. He wanted to buy them.

"Neither one of them wanted the other one to get any type of advantage over them. It was just so important to them to win that game."

Ohio State 12, Michigan 10

1974: Michigan arrived at The Horseshoe with another 10–0 record. The Buckeyes were 9–1, with a loss to Michigan State. The Wolverines missed another last-gasp field-goal attempt and Ohio State's fans stormed the field to tear down the goal posts.

Ohio State 21, Michigan 14

1975: Neither team owned a loss when the two sides clashed at Michigan Stadium, but Schembechler's squad had two ties. The Buckeyes scored a pair of touchdowns in the final few minutes to erase a seven-point deficit and to snap Michigan's 41-game home-field winning streak.

Michigan 22, Ohio State 0

1976: Both teams entered with a 9–1 mark, but Michigan scored all of the game's points in the second half en route to the most lopsided result of the decade-long battle.

Michigan 14, Ohio State 6

1977: Ohio State went another year without reaching the end zone against its rival, as the Michigan defense held tight on a decisive fourth down with a minute remaining.

Michigan 14, Ohio State 3

1978: For the third consecutive season, the Buckeyes were held without a touchdown in the rivalry game. Ohio State grabbed an early 3–0 lead, but failed to score the rest of the contest.

* * *

Schembechler's ties to Woody and to Ohio State made the rivalry extra personal. He said he would "never forget how tough that guy was." Overall, during the 10 years of warfare, Michigan came out on top five times. Ohio State won four of the meetings. The teams tied once.

"I never brought it up when I coached, but I have close ties at Ohio State," Schembechler said. "Unfortunately, I even have a graduate degree from there. They made me go to school while I was a graduate assistant.

"I have enormous, enormous respect for Ohio State. Enormous. That's why I loved to play them when I was up there. There's no other team I would rather play, no other coach I would rather go against than the old man."

Cherish the Streak

Bill Long can laugh about it now. He sets his fork down next to his slice of pumpkin pie, takes a sip of his coffee, and sits back in his wooden chair. That football, the one he stuffed into his locker after the 1969 Rose Bowl, it makes him smile now. More than four decades have passed, and that time has soothed Long's conscience. The grudge he held toward his coaches for being relegated to the sideline for most of Ohio State's undefeated season in 1968—it has decreased in intensity over the years.

Long took the majority of the snaps for the first four games of what developed into a school-record 22-game winning streak. In 1968, however, as Ohio State rattled off 10 more victories and established itself as the nation's top team, Long watched Rex Kern conduct the offense from under center.

For a while, Long could not stand it. Following the Buckeyes' triumph against USC in that Rose Bowl, when head coach Woody Hayes presented him with a game ball for his leadership and help with preparation, Long shoved the football into his locker and never looked back.

Then, more than four decades later, Urban Meyer's Buckeyes caught up to that long-standing record. And as Meyer's team eclipsed that 22-game streak, Long finally accepted his college football fate. He became much more relaxed, much more at ease, and much more aware of his involvement in a historic era of Ohio State football.

He is at peace, at leisure. After all, who else eats pie for lunch?

"I find it fascinating," Long said of Meyer's team, which rattled off 24 consecutive victories before falling to Michigan State in the 2013 Big Ten Championship Game. "That's unreal."

Urban Meyer took a team that had its first losing season since 1988 in 2011 and, against the odds, led it to a 24-game winning streak over two seasons.

Meyer grabbed the reins of a program that lost seven games in 2011—the team's first losing season since 1988—and faced a bowl ban in 2012. Somehow, he steered the Buckeyes to an unbeaten year in his first season at the helm. He did not experience defeat until his 25th contest as boss in Columbus. Those who played on the teams in the late '60s did not mind seeing their record broken. Michigan snapped Ohio State's 22-game win streak with a 24–12 victory in Ann Arbor, Michigan, in the final week of the 1969 regular season.

"I am a Buckeye. I went to school there," said Earle Bruce, an assistant coach on Hayes' staff in the late '60s. "I played there. I coached there. I was an assistant, a head coach. I'm for anything that's better than we had. I'm for any record breaking, anything."

Kern tunes in to the Buckeyes each Saturday from his home in California. He was most impressed with the team's ability to keep its head above water, despite never-ending scrutiny, a nonstop news cycle, and constant distractions on social media.

"I'm delighted and thrilled," Kern said. "Anyone thinking short of that is not a real, true, loyal Buckeye fan. As a former player, I take that as a compliment that people [compare] Urban's team and what he has done to our team. It's wonderful to be remembered that way."

Long also appreciates the comparisons between the eras, though he admitted to an initial feeling of uneasiness about the surpassing of his group's record.

"Inside, there is a feeling of, 'Oh, shoot, I hope that doesn't happen,'" Long said. "But there is a rational thing of, 'That's life.' Records are made to be broken. I think most people understand that change happens."

Until the new streak approached 20 games and reporters began asking players about it, many members of the team had no idea that it existed.

"It is crazy," said center Corey Linsley. "It's not surprising, though, because of how hard we've worked."

In 1967, after a last-second loss dropped Ohio State to 2–3, Long directed the team to four straight victories to close out the season. That set the tone for the Buckeyes, who opened the 1968 campaign as the No. 11 team in the nation. After a shutout win against top-ranked Purdue in mid-October, voters vaulted the Buckeyes to No. 2. Ohio State capped its perfect season with a 50–14 win against Michigan and a 27–16 win against USC. Hayes' bunch remained at No. 1 for nearly the duration of the 1969 season. The group outscored its first eight opponents 371–69 before the streak perished in the finale against Michigan.

To Kern, that loss overshadowed everything the Buckeyes had accomplished. It still stings. Meyer's team kicked itself too, once its streak ended against the Spartans. A win in the conference title game would have likely vaulted the Buckeyes into the national championship game.

Still, both teams pieced together incredible, historic streaks. Long does not know what happened to that football he abandoned that one day. Maybe a janitor stumbled upon it and placed it on a shelf somewhere. Maybe it has its own listing on eBay. Maybe it is still at the bottom of that locker. Either way, he and his former teammates appreciated the opportunity to reflect on a storied era of Ohio State football. Similar to Meyer's team, the group from the late '60s, under the guidance of a stern, no-nonsense coach, approached each game like a championship battle.

One thing is for certain: both teams made winning look easy.

Easy as pie.

Jump into Mirror Lake

Long before students treated it like a bathtub, Mirror Lake was a source of drinking water for Ohio State's campus. Well, find a water fountain or grab a bottle of Aquafina the week of the Michigan game.

Since 1990, students, alumni, and penguins have flocked to the center of campus and plunged into the frigid, little pond. OK, there are no penguins. But no one would blink twice at the sight of the black and white birds, given how cold it typically is in late November in Columbus. The tradition began the Thursday before Ohio State's tilt with rival Michigan that year. The rivalry game is always the last game of the regular season. Once the Big Ten expanded two decades later, however, "The Game" was pushed back a week on the schedule to the Saturday after Thanksgiving. That would have required students to jump in the lake with bellies full of turkey, but since most students head home for the holiday, the custom was moved to the Tuesday before the affair.

The Mirror Lake Jump is not a university-sanctioned event, but in 2013, the school placed a fence around the area for the day of the jump and required wristbands for entry. The first jump drew fewer than 100 people to the artificial lake. In 2014, nearly 15,000 braved the wintry conditions.

Some students ignore the typically frigid temperatures and descend into the brutally cold water while wearing a bathing suit or a T-shirt. Many secure their shoes or flip flops onto their feet with duct tape; it can be a long, miserable walk back to the dorm room or apartment if one's shoes get jarred loose and sink to the bottom of the lake. Each year, some students are treated for cuts, scrapes, or sprains. Some come down with an illness of some sort. A large contingent of students merely stand and watch the sandless arctic beach party. Some clutch the keys and phones of their water-bound friends.

In the end, the scene resembles something out of Woodstock, only on a smaller scale and with more hypothermia. Students do not just venture to the lake, dip their toes in the water, turn around, and head home. They soak in the water and take pictures with friends. They shout the lyrics to "We Don't Give a Damn for the Whole State of Michigan." They wave scarlet and gray flags.

A handful of students usually jump into the lake the night before the scheduled event, just to beat the masses to the punch. There always seem to be one or two stooges who cannonball into the water amid the afternoon's broad daylight, with students and staff passing by en route to class or work. Special events can also trigger an impromptu mass jump. When the United States government announced the capture of Osama bin Laden on May 1, 2011, students rushed to the lake with American flags. The area was mobbed until the wee hours of the morning. Jumping into the lake is technically a fourth-degree misdemeanor, but police do not enforce that mandate the night of the tradition.

The sun rises the next day, and sitting at the bottom of the lake—where serenity reigns in the wake of the previous night's madness—are hundreds of student ID cards, keys, shoes, glasses, wallets, phones, shirts, hats, rings, necklaces, bracelets, earrings, hair ties, and wristbands. On several occasions, the university has cleaned out the lake and restored it, only to find a litany of bizarre objects at the bottom, such as a broom, an orthopedic foot brace, a microwave, a dining hall tray, a dog toy, a beach ball, a mattress, a golf ball, a wine glass, a Frisbee, and a traffic cone. The university typically spends upward of $20,000 to clean up the lake and surrounding area each year following the jump.

University archives suggest that in 1964, an engaged couple got into a tiff. The woman removed her engagement ring while the two argued and the man grabbed it and heaved it into the lake. The next day, the woman, clad in a raincoat, scuba mask, and a bikini, went for a dip in an attempt to find the ring. Swimming in the lake was prohibited, but police permitted her to embark on her search. She located the ring and eventually married her fiancé.

When students are not spreading their germs in the water, Mirror Lake is a pristine landmark on Ohio State's campus. A student organization has held "Light up the Lake" each year since 2003, an event in which volunteers decorate the trees encompassing Mirror Lake with holiday lights. During a tree-lighting ceremony, those in attendance sing a rendition of "Carmen Ohio."

A fountain near the east end of the lake sprays water in the air. Ducks make their home in the water once spring arrives. Students often populate the benches—gifted by the class of 1981—and walls around the lake when the weather permits. It can be a peaceful place to study or read a book or people watch. The Browning Amphitheatre, a large block of stone seating, has hosted concerts, ceremonies, and presentations through the years.

The School of Music performs its annual spring concert series at the location and, in 1910, the first marching band concert was played there. In its early state, Mirror Lake was just a ravine that flowed from High Street to the Olentangy River. Now, the lake holds nearly 100,000 cubic feet of water and has a brick floor and concrete sides. The graduating class of 2005 devoted their group gift to the "beautification of Mirror Lake."

For a While

Rex Kern did not need to hear the rest of the question. Minutes after finishing lunch with his wife, Nancy, at their California home, the former Ohio State quarterback reminisced about his college career, his playing days under Woody Hayes, and the near-dynasty the group established. He was then asked to navigate one of the darker passageways in his brain, one filled with memories of a haunting Saturday afternoon from nearly a half-century earlier.

That day in Ann Arbor, Michigan, the Buckeyes' final stop before a seemingly inevitable national title game appearance, did not unfold so seamlessly.

So, did that loss to Michigan sting for a while? When did it…

"For a while?" Kern yelled.

That defeat, one in which Kern tossed four interceptions…

"For a while?" Kern repeated.

That unshakeable disappointment, which snapped a 22-game winning streak…

"For a while?" Kern shouted again. "How about for a lifetime?"

The 24–12 loss to their archnemesis forever tormented Kern and the rest of the 1969 Ohio State team.

"It still lingers," said running back Jim Otis. "It still bothers me."

Only twice during a three-year stretch from 1968 to 1970 did Ohio State fall short on the scoreboard. And yet, Kern joked he should contact Ohio State's psychology department to analyze why, for the longest time, he could only reflect back on the two defeats: the 1969

Michigan game and a loss to Stanford in the Rose Bowl the following season.

"Those two losses, obviously, cost us two national championships," Kern said. "Those were extremely disappointing losses."

Not until he sat in the stands at Sun Devil Stadium in Tempe, Arizona, on January 3, 2003, did Kern learn to appreciate the 22-game streak and the 1968 national title. For 35 years, he had dwelled on the two defeats. When he watched his alma mater capture the sport's ultimate triumph against a heavily favored Miami team, he learned to appreciate what he had accomplished.

"I never had a chance to reflect back on it and appreciate what we did, because I think of those two losses," Kern said. "And then when we won it all, Woody was not going to let us sit back and say, 'Hey, look what we did. This is wonderful.' So I never had a chance to experience it until I was at the national championship game when Jim Tressel and Craig Krenzel and those guys won it. It finally hit me that this is something special. Even though we won one, there are a lot of teams in the country that would love to have one and we could have and should have had three."

The Buckeyes spent the entire 1969 regular season as the top-ranked team in the nation. They outscored their first eight opponents by more than 300 points. Kern surmised that they developed a sense of complacency and invincibility, given that their smallest margin of victory was 27 points. A year earlier, when they went 10–0 and captured the national title, they sweated out half of their wins by 13 points or fewer. After the first quarter of Ohio State's season-opening 62–0 dismantling of Texas Christian, defensive back Jack Tatum, typically hush, approached Kern and said, "Rex, stop scoring so fast and so much. We're on the field more than you guys are on the field. We need a break."

The season before, against USC in the Rose Bowl, the de facto national title game, the Buckeyes fell behind 10–0. Kern entered the huddle and deployed the threat of an angry Woody Hayes as motivation.

"You seniors, you are done with the old man," Kern told his teammates. "But we have to ride back on the airplane with him and we have two more years. It is not going to be a happy plane ride back, so let's get after it."

That sort of provocation worked in 1968. The Buckeyes, though, lacked that impetus in 1969. They shooed away No. 10 Purdue 42–14 on November 15. A week later, they crumbled against the rival Wolverines and first-year coach Bo Schembechler in what became the first installment of the storied Ten Year War between the two schools. Michigan entered the affair with a 7–2 record and the nation's No. 12 ranking.

"Whenever a team wins so easily and the point spread is so great," Kern said, "when you get into a tight ball game, even though it might be tied or you might be behind by maybe a field goal, you start thinking, 'Holy cow, we're getting beat.' And you start pressing."

Kern threw four interceptions. In all, Ohio State committed seven turnovers. Michigan also returned a punt 60 yards to the Buckeyes' 3-yard line.

"It's Woody Hayes' Football 101: you can't turn the ball over," Otis said. "You can't make mental errors. That game was a great illustration of that. We could have all had Superman outfits on and gone up there and there is no way we could have won that game with the [mistakes]."

The errors still eat at guys like Kern and Otis. So does the thought of what could have been.

"The Michigan guys talk about how they really took it to us," Otis said. "Let me tell you something: I could still play against them. I could get out there right now and run over their asses."

Time does not always heal the deepest wounds. Just ask Kern.

Not for a while, though. The memory still burns.

Chapter 4

Memorable Seasons

Remember the Season of Dreams

Be it a fairy tale or Hollywood drama, there must be a reasonable amount of reality involved. The script must be believable. David defeats Goliath once, not over and over again. Otherwise, David would be the heralded character, not Goliath, and no one would be surprised at another one of David's victory parades. Any screenplay writer, though, can build to a compelling final showdown between the two parties by making David look as vulnerable as possible along the way and by preserving the power and mystique of Goliath, a seemingly immortal figure. That sequence played out in 2002.

Ohio State entered the 2003 Fiesta Bowl—the national championship icing atop the regular-season cake—as David. Miami steamrolled its way to Tempe, Arizona, having rattled off 34 consecutive victories. Enter Goliath, stage right. This was no ordinary bout between a longshot and a heavyweight, though. The Buckeyes flirted with disaster throughout their journey to January's final tilt. Sure, they needed to overcome the odds—which placed them as nearly a two-touchdown underdog against the mighty Hurricanes—to claim the crystal football. But all season, they had been shocking and awing with the way they navigated a tightrope. Few teams have ever eked out so many narrow victories and maintained an unblemished record.

Maybe that is why the Buckeyes entered the Fiesta Bowl with so much confidence. They knew that if the battle morphed into a war of attrition, they could yank another late-game rabbit out of their bottomless hat. Maybe being publicly perceived as facing such a daunting task relieved the team of any external sources of pressure. No one expected them to win, so Miami held the weight of the nation on its shoulders.

Whatever the reason, Ohio State arrived at Sun Devil Stadium expected to serve as merely the next victim for a Hurricanes squad eyeing a second straight national title. Those in the Buckeyes' locker room thought differently. But the national perspective just assumed Miami would roll over this team that won six of its 13 regular-season games by seven points or fewer. In fact, defensive lineman Kenny Peterson was asked by a reporter five days before the contest: "Are you confident you're going to win this game?"

Would any competitor ever admit to feeling the contrary, no matter the circumstances?

"Of course," Peterson replied. "You don't want to go into a fight saying, 'I'm going to lose.' Of course you've got confidence going into any game, no matter [if you're] playing Playstation or football."

Later in the press conference, linebacker Matt Wilhelm was asked, in relation to the overwhelming media attention all week, about the silliest question he had received. Wilhelm pointed to the question Peterson had been asked moments earlier.

"That was the weirdest thing," Peterson said.

"Do we feel confident we're going to win?" Wilhelm said. "I don't think if any of us were not confident, we would have ever gotten on a plane to come to Tempe."

That sentiment was not limited to Wilhelm. Freshman running back Maurice Clarett was asked about Miami's team speed. He did not sugarcoat in his response.

"You don't go 'Wow,'" Clarett said. "Everybody puts their pants on the same way. Anything can happen that day."

Despite what prognosticators projected, despite the uncomfortable ride Ohio State took to reach the title game, despite the perceived difference in size, speed, talent, and recent history, the Buckeyes did not consider themselves to be at a disadvantage. Two unbeaten teams remained. Sixty minutes of football—well, 60 and change, since the

PHEW!

The number of narrow escapes the Buckeyes executed during the 2002 season made their march to a national championship all the more impressive and implausible. Here is a breakdown of the close calls along the way to the title.

September 21: Ohio State 23, Cincinnati 19

The numbers: The Bearcats outgained the Buckeyes, 415 yards to 292, including a 324-to-129 edge in passing yardage. Ohio State's Craig Krenzel completed only 14 of 29 passes for 129 yards, with two touchdowns and two interceptions. Cincinnati's Gino Guidugli completed 26 of 52 pass attempts for 324 yards, with one touchdown and two picks. Ohio State running back Lydell Ross totaled 130 yards on the ground on 23 carries.

The skinny: Cincinnati grabbed a 9–0 lead, as the Buckeyes went punt, punt, punt, fumble, interception on their five first-quarter drives. Krenzel scored on a six-yard scamper with a little less than four minutes remaining to give Ohio State a 23–19 lead. In the final minute, the Bearcats moved the ball to the Buckeyes' 15-yard line, but Guidugli heaved three consecutive incomplete passes before firing a fourth-down pass into the grasp of Ohio State defensive back Will Allen. The Buckeyes took a knee and let out a sigh of relief.

The quote: "It sucks. It sucks so bad. You take nothing from a loss, not a damn thing," Guidugli said. "It hurts, hurts so bad. We had the No. 6 team in the country on the ropes and we couldn't knock them out."

October 19: Ohio State 19, Wisconsin 14

The numbers: The Buckeyes and Badgers matched wits for most of the game. Ohio State totaled 382 yards; Wisconsin amassed 340. Both teams ran 63 plays on offense. Ohio State piled up 178 rushing yards;

Wisconsin gained 180. Both teams ran the ball 44 times. Krenzel completed 12 of 19 passes. Three players combined for 11 completions in 19 attempts for Wisconsin. Freshman running back Maurice Clarett gained 133 yards on the ground for Ohio State.

The skinny: The Buckeyes seemed poised to blow past the Badgers, as they took the game's opening possession 75 yards for a touchdown in three plays, as Krenzel connected with receiver Michael Jenkins on a 47-yard score. The well ran dry pretty quickly, though. Wisconsin carried a 14–13 lead into the fourth quarter, but Krenzel hooked up with tight end Ben Hartsock for a three-yard touchdown with 10 minutes remaining. A failed two-point conversion kept the score at 19–14. The Badgers had two more chances, but quarterback Jim Sorgi tossed an interception at the Ohio State 20-yard line and then Wisconsin went three-and-out with five minutes left and the Buckeyes ran out the clock.

The quote: "I was catching that with every part of my body possible," Hartsock said. "It was like there was a baby in there."

October 26: Ohio State 13, Penn State 7

The numbers: Ohio State's defense limited the Nittany Lions to 179 total yards and only eight first downs. The teams combined for seven turnovers, one of which defined the game. Penn State quarterback Zack Mills completed 14 of 28 passes for 98 yards and three interceptions. Krenzel went 13 of 20 for 112 yards and two picks.

The skinny: There was not much offense in the affair. The Nittany Lions gripped a 7–3 lead until the first drive of the fourth quarter, when Buckeyes cornerback Chris Gamble nabbed an errant Mills toss and returned it 38 yards for Ohio State's only touchdown of the afternoon.

The quote: "I saw Zack Mills rolling to the left, the one dude running the post and the other dude running the wheel [route]," Gamble said. "I saw him throw it to the wheel, and I just attacked it."

November 9: Ohio State 10, Purdue 6

The numbers: Purdue outgained Ohio State, 341 to 267, but the Boilermakers turned the ball over on three occasions. The Buckeyes only gave it away once. Purdue quarterback Kyle Orton threw three interceptions. Clarett was the Buckeyes' leading rusher, with only 52 yards.

The skinny: In one of the most memorable games in Ohio State history, the Buckeyes turned a 6–3 deficit into a 10–6 victory with one gutsy fourth-down call with about two minutes remaining. Needing about a yard and a half, Krenzel stepped up in the pocket and hit Jenkins in stride for a 37-yard score.

The quote: "We're not going to drop in the Big Ten standings, and that is what's important right now," Ohio State head coach Jim Tressel said.

November 16: Ohio State 23, Illinois 16 (OT)

The numbers: Illinois ran 14 more plays (80 to 66) and racked up 37 more yards than Ohio State. Krenzel completed only 10 passes for 176 yards. Six of those completions and 147 of those yards came on tosses to Jenkins, including a 50-yard touchdown early in the third quarter. Fighting Illini quarterback Jon Beutjer threw for 305 yards, with 27 completions in 45 attempts. The Buckeyes, without Clarett, who was out with a stinger, relied on Ross and Maurice Hall to shoulder the load in the backfield. The two combined for 120 yards on 32 carries.

The skinny: The teams traded field goals for much of the afternoon, though Ohio State's typically reliable kicker, Mike Nugent, missed a pair of attempts, including one from 41 yards midway through the fourth quarter. That kept the score at 16–13, in the Buckeyes' favor. After a furious rally downfield in the final minute, which included a fourth-down conversion, Illinois kicker John Gockman tucked a 48-yard field goal just inside the left upright as time expired to send the game into overtime. Krenzel scrambled to his left and rushed 14 yards on third-and-10 on the opening possession of the extra period. Hall later scored from eight yards out. Illinois proceeded to push the ball to the Buckeyes' 9-yard line, but Beutjer threw three straight incompletions and the Buckeyes prevailed. Receiver Aaron Moorehead hauled in a fade pass lofted over the top of defensive back Dustin Fox on second down, but he could not plant his left foot in bounds. On third down, Walter Young appeared to snag a perfectly placed toss in the left corner of the end zone, but the official ruled Young had bobbled the catch. Beutjer stood, hands on hips, in disbelief. Beutjer's last gasp was batted down at the line of scrimmage.

The quote: "Nobody said winning the Big Ten championship would be easy," Jenkins said.

November 23: Ohio State 14, Michigan 9
The numbers: Michigan totaled 368 yards of offense and the Wolverines limited Ohio State to only 264. Michigan ran 89 plays and Ohio State ran only 48. The Wolverines tallied 26 first downs. The Buckeyes only notched 13. Michigan also turned the ball over twice. Ohio State protected the football. Both Braylon Edwards and Ronald Bellamy eclipsed 100 yards receiving. Clarett gained 119 yards and scored a touchdown.

The skinny: Michigan carried a 9–7 lead into intermission after a 19-play, 88-yard drive capped with a short field goal at the end of the second quarter. The teams traded punts until Hall scooted three yards to the end zone with five minutes remaining. Michigan quarterback John Navarre engineered a desperate rally, but he was picked off by Allen near the end zone to seal the 14–9 final score.

The quote: "We might not go out and score 50 points," Clarett said. "We might not hold teams to 10 yards. But we make the plays when we have to."

sides eventually required a pair of overtime periods—would decide their fate, not all of the one-sided breakdowns etched on paper.

Offensive coordinator Jim Bollman contended that he would not prepare for the game any differently, whether his squad was a three-touchdown favorite or a five-touchdown underdog. Defensive coordinator Mark Dantonio said the Buckeyes stepped onto the field expecting to win, not hoping. Clarett said he embraced the widespread doubt.

"You have nothing to lose and everything to gain," he said. "It gives you more incentive to fight [harder] on every play."

No play better represented that idea than when Clarett chased down Miami safety Sean Taylor in the third quarter and ripped the football from his paws.

Thanks to three Miami turnovers, the Buckeyes—before a mostly scarlet-clad crowd—carried a 14–7 lead into halftime. They threatened to extend that edge to two touchdowns, but quarterback Craig Krenzel, a molecular genetics major and heady signal-caller, fired an interception in the end zone. Taylor snagged the errant pass and returned it about 30 yards before Clarett came from behind and wrestled the ball away. Ohio State tacked on a field goal to attain a 17–7 advantage.

"Krenzel did for us what we needed done," Tressel said. "He led the team, fought like crazy, he made plays, most especially when they had to be made. He's tough. Probably the No. 1 characteristic that a quarterback better have, especially a quarterback at Ohio State, [is] he better be tough. He's tough. He played tough."

Miami running back Willis McGahee plunged into the end zone from nine yards out to narrow the Hurricanes' deficit, but his night ended shortly after that score. Early in the fourth quarter, Will Allen jarred McGahee's knee with his shoulder on a tackle. McGahee's knee was torn to shreds. Miami managed without him, though. The Hurricanes converted a 40-yard field goal as time ran out in regulation. The teams headed to overtime.

Hurricanes quarterback Ken Dorsey connected with tight end Kellen Winslow Jr. for a seven-yard touchdown to commence the extra period. After a penalty, a sack, and an incompletion, the Buckeyes faced a fourth-and-14 from the 29-yard line. Krenzel hooked up with lanky receiver Michael Jenkins for a 17-yard gain to stave off defeat. A few plays later, they encountered a fourth-and-3. Krenzel slung a pass for receiver Chris Gamble in the right corner of the end zone, but the ball caromed off of Gamble's hands and was deemed incomplete. A sea of green and orange spilled out onto the field.

Krenzel was hit as he released the pass. He claimed to have seen some contact between Gamble and defensive back Glenn Sharpe in the corner of the end zone, but he did not see a yellow flag fall to the ground.

"The ball fell incomplete and their team rushed the field," Krenzel said, "and I sat there and, to be honest, it was a feeling of dejection, thinking the game was over, knowing how hard we played and how much effort we put in, and just at that time thinking we weren't victorious. I thought there was contact, but I didn't see the flag until after I got up."

Ohio State head coach Jim Tressel did not immediately see field judge Terry Porter pull the flag from his pocket, either.

"I thought, 'Isn't that a shame?'" Tressel said.

Porter tossed the flag. The defibrillator worked. The Buckeyes had new life. First-and-goal from the 2-yard line.

Porter later said he saw Sharpe holding Gamble prior to Krenzel launching the football into orbit. He said Sharpe kept holding him and "pulling him down while the ball was in the air." He replayed the sequence in his mind for confirmation before he decided to issue a penalty.

Krenzel plowed into the end zone on third down. Ohio State sent the game into a second overtime. Clarett plunged into pay dirt to put Ohio State in front 31–24. That heavy favorite, the team that had not lost in 846 days, was looking eye to eye with a historic upset. They converted a fourth-and-3 and plodded along to Ohio State's 1-yard line. On fourth-and-goal, Dorsey heaved the ball up for grabs as he was struck by linebacker Cie Grant. The pass fell incomplete.

They did it. David outlasted Goliath.

"It's still unbelievable to hear those fireworks go off and rush the field," said safety and team captain Mike Doss. "We won the game but it was the game on the national stage, two overtimes. We're sitting here looking at each other. We're little kids in the candy store. It's Christmas for us."

Underdogs? In theory, perhaps.

"Our guys had every confidence going into the football game, that we would compete," Tressel said. "We knew they were a great football team and we had not played them before, so you didn't know for sure exactly what the matchup would [produce]. I would say it was a pretty even matchup. Two great heavyweights slugging it out. We came up with the win. Our guys had every confidence we had that ability."

Quite simply, the Buckeyes shocked the world. They survived a slew of regular-season scares, emerging victorious each time an opponent threatened their unblemished record. When the stage grew in size, they stood taller. The perfect season exceeded any expectations even the most idealistic Buckeyes fans could have anticipated.

"I don't think the most avid, unrealistic Ohio State fan who thinks we're never ever going to lose again, in their wildest dreams, would have thought that they would go 14–0 in their second year under Tressel," said Ohio State football historian Jack Park.

Along the way, the Buckeyes kept suspense high, narrowly escaping the jaws of defeat on a number of occasions. There was the four-point win against Cincinnati at Paul Brown Stadium, on the banks of the Ohio River, in late September. A last-gasp pass attempt to the end zone by Bearcats quarterback Gino Guidugli fell into Allen's grasp. There was the five-point win at raucous Camp Randall Stadium in Madison, Wisconsin, where the Buckeyes scored the go-ahead touchdown in the fourth quarter and ran out the final four and a half minutes of game clock. There was the six-point win against Penn State in the last week of October, a victory secured thanks to a pick-six by Gamble. There was the 10–6 triumph against Purdue in West Lafayette, Indiana, on November 9, a game decided on a fourth-down prayer-and-heave by Krenzel with less than two minutes remaining. There was the overtime victory one week later in Champaign, Illinois, against a scrappy Illinois team. There was the five-point win against archenemy Michigan, a victory recorded the instant John Navarre's pass sailed into the arms of Allen, who stepped in front of receiver Braylon Edwards in front of the goal line as the clock displayed a trio of zeroes.

All told, it was an exhausting march to Tempe. By the time the Buckeyes pulled off their final heroic feat, Tressel felt as wistful and nostalgic as he did jubilant.

"When you end a year like we did in '02," he said, "with that group that had transitioned together and had grown to love one another and compete like crazy, it was a little bit melancholy after the game, the fact that we were never going to be together in that fashion."

Ohio State regularly draws more than 105,000 fans to The Horseshoe for home football games.

Attend a Game at The Shoe

Keith Jackson's voice still rings loud and clear. "On the banks of the Olentangy," the play-by-play announcer used to say during his introduction to any game at Ohio Stadium. The landmark building rests adjacent to the shores of the river that meanders through Columbus. Ohio Stadium serves as the constitutional beacon of campus. Only a parking lot and some shrubbery separate the venue's west end from the flowing river. The stadium itself is a short walk from the central part of campus, where students attend class and can peer out windows and see the massive, scarlet "O" that adorns the south end. The football team's home, opened in 1922, truly is Howard Dwight Smith's finest work.

On October 21, 1922, the critics were hushed. Chic Harley had changed everything. The Buckeyes had played their home affairs at Ohio Field, a structure on the east side of campus that could host about 14,000 fans. Harley, a star halfback, directed Ohio State to

Western Conference championships in 1916 and 1917. As a result, the demand for tickets skyrocketed. Fans would pack Ohio Field to capacity and large gatherings would populate the place's perimeter. Some fans even watched the action from the rooftops of nearby buildings.

Naturally, the idea for a new, more sizable venue began to catch on. Smith, an Ohio State alumnus and a renowned, respected architect, was recruited to captain the development of the project. But when Ohio Stadium finally opened in 1922 with a seating capacity of about 63,000, some remained skeptical. Could the place really sell out?

The stadium, after a year-long construction that cost about $1.3 million, debuted for Ohio State's tilt against Ohio Wesleyan on October 7. Two weeks later, when Michigan came to town, more than 71,000 fans overfilled the stands. Ohio Stadium was dedicated that day with a 21-gun salute before the Buckeyes fell to the Wolverines 19–0.

Smith later served as the university architect and became responsible for a slew of buildings that still stand on campus. Ohio Stadium, though, was his crown jewel. For his efforts, Smith was awarded a gold medal from the American Institute of Architects. The National Park Service added the structure to the National Register of Historic Places in 1974. By 2014, its seating capacity had risen to nearly 105,000, making it the third-largest football stadium in the country. It regularly welcomes more than 108,000 for a Saturday contest.

"It's the toughest place to play, by far, because of the intensity of the crowd," former Michigan coach Bo Schembechler once said.

Of course, Ohio Stadium's distinctive shape remains its separating factor. The open end beyond the south end zone supplied the place with the nickname "The Horseshoe." The building was the first horseshoe-shaped, double-deck stadium in the nation. Over time, the open end on the south side became enclosed as the university added more—and permanent—seating. By the beginning of the 2001 campaign, after a $194 million renovation initiative, the stadium

SEA OF SCARLET

The Buckeyes always feel welcomed by the home crowd at Ohio Stadium. They often feel comfortable in front of thousands of scarlet-clad fans on the road, too. Ohio State supporters are known to travel well. When the Buckeyes captured the national championship in Tempe, Arizona, on January 3, 2003, they celebrated with a stadium mostly filled with fans in Ohio State gear.

"Every time we go to a stadium, we have at lot of Buckeye fans," said head coach Jim Tressel. "This one, it felt like a home game. It really did. They have a way of getting tickets to other people's venues. You can't even plug into the formula what percent of impact they had. They had a hand in it. With that more important than the one play, them being there, maybe that was the play, you know, that turned the game on before the game even started. Our fans are extraordinary and they care about their school. They care about their players. They care about how our players play, and I think they really appreciate our players."

Following the 2007 regular season, the Buckeyes ventured to Louisiana to square off against LSU. The teams clashed at the Superdome in New Orleans, a little more than an hour from LSU's campus in Baton Rouge. Even then, Tressel did not expect too much of a disadvantage from a support standpoint.

"I expect our people to have gotten as many tickets as they could possibly get their hands on," he said a couple of days before the game. "How many that is, I don't know. You know, maybe a third of the group. I don't know. But I expect it to be very electric, which is a great thing. I think you can feed off the energy. The way I look at it, I don't know if they're cheering for me or against me, but they're cheering. So that's electricity, and I expect it to be a lot of fun."

Ohio State lost the game 38–24, but Ohio State fans did, in fact, show up in full force. They filled the stadium at the Fiesta Bowl against Notre Dame in 2006 and in Glendale, Arizona, a year later, when the Buckeyes lost to Florida in the title game. Against LSU, playing in the Tigers' backyard, they still made their presence felt.

"I think you can take things for granted at times," Tressel said. "But the Buckeye fans and everyone that surrounds us, you can feel that they are not taking something like this for granted, because it's a special opportunity and I'm sure that there would be about 50,000 more of them here if they could have rounded up tickets."

Michigan's attendance had declined a bit in the 1960s, as the Wolverines suffered five losing seasons in a nine-year span under head coach Bump Elliott.

"They played a lot of games up there with 50,000 people in the stands," said Ohio State football historian Jack Park. "The stadium was half full."

Upon the arrival of head coach Bo Schembechler in 1969, Michigan started to draw between 60,000-75,000 fans per home game, Park said. On the Monday before the annual affair between Ohio State and Michigan, the Wolverines had somewhere between 20,000-25,000 unsold tickets. Under the instruction of athletic director Don Canham, Will Perry, the team's sports information director from 1968 to 1980, loaded up a station wagon with all of the unsold tickets and hauled them down to the Ohio State ticket office. All of the Columbus radio stations and newspapers sent out messages that fans in the area could still corral tickets to that Saturday's contest. When the undefeated Buckeyes strolled into Michigan Stadium on that Saturday afternoon, they did so before a then-record 103,588 fans. A fairly sized portion of them traveled from Columbus.

"Basically, the Ohio State fans sold out that game," Park said. "There had never been a sellout until that game."

could hold upward of 99,000 and the open end was all but a thing of the past.

The field itself has also undergone a series of modifications over the years. Natural grass was replaced with Astroturf in 1972 to support the Buckeyes' annually potent rushing attack. The material became known as "Woody's Carpet," an ode to head coach Woody Hayes. In 1990, however, after the turf took a toll on the players' limbs, the stadium reverted to grass. In 2007, the team installed FieldTurf.

Upon its debut, Ohio Stadium featured wooden signs operated by hand for scoreboards. In 1984, a digital scoreboard—one that cost more than the original foundation of the entire stadium—was installed.

Ohio State led the nation in attendance each year from 1958 to 1971. Since 1949, the school has never ranked lower than fourth in the country in average home game attendance. Each Saturday, fans gather near the north end, a daunting rotunda that resembles a Roman coliseum. Drivers can spot the massive concrete structure as they whiz past on Route 315. The school logo, adorning the back of the scoreboard, can be seen from a distance on campus. With pillars that seemingly touch the clouds and an oval-like shape, the structure is a bit intimidating. But it is mostly intimidating for the opponents who must play in it, with more than 100,000 fans howling in their scarlet jerseys.

· ·

The Buckeyes were reeling. They had gained a little more than 200 yards on a lackluster Saturday afternoon. They had failed to reach the end zone against a Purdue team saddled with a losing record. Their national championship hopes were fading into the gray skies above Ross-Ade Stadium in West Lafayette, Indiana. Their sparkling record—10–0 on the morning of November 9, 2002—appeared to be in serious jeopardy.

Then, as play-by-play announcer Brent Musberger shouted: "Touchdown! Touchdown! Michael Jenkins! On fourth-and-1! Would you believe it? Craig Krenzel strikes with a minute and a half left. Holy Buckeye!"

With about two and a half minutes remaining and the Boilermakers gripping a 6–3 advantage, Ohio State quarterback Craig Krenzel completed a pass to tight end Ben Hartsock on third-and-14. The completion gained about 12 and a half yards and positioned the Buckeyes at the 37-yard line. They trailed by three and needed a little more than a yard as the clock ticked to under two minutes. The Buckeyes had no choice: they had to go for it.

"Purdue's defense [seemed] to think that we were running," Krenzel said. "I would probably think that on fourth and 1. I was throwing into the wind."

Star freshman running back Maurice Clarett was bothered by a shoulder stinger. He remained on the sideline. Krenzel lined up under center. Lydell Ross stood, hands on his knees, in the backfield. Ohio State split one receiver out wide on each end. Michael Jenkins streaked down the left side of the field. Chris Gamble ran an underneath route.

Krenzel dropped back about eight yards. As the pocket around him collapsed, he took a few steps forward to buy Jenkins some extra time to gain separation. He was throwing it deep. He was going for the home run, the game-winner.

Tressel eventually wrote in his book, *The Winners Manual: For the Game of Life*, that his initial reaction to Krenzel throwing deep was along the lines of "What? We just need two yards. Oh no, no."

His expression swiftly changed.

"When the ball was caught in the end zone for a touchdown, my 'Oh no,' turned into, 'Yes!'"

Jenkins hauled in Krenzel's heave just as he glided across the goal line.

"That's what a receiver has to do," Jenkins said. "We have to separate when the ball is coming."

Jenkins flipped the ball to the referee and then Gamble, in celebratory fashion, tackled his teammate to the ground. The rest of the offensive unit sprinted down the field to embrace the receiver. Musberger shouted: "People said all year, 'At some time, Craig Krenzel would have to win a game.' And on fourth-and-1, he goes 37 yards." The season-saving miracle preserved Ohio State's unblemished record. Gamble grabbed an interception on Purdue's final possession to secure the victory.

"It's a situation I wish everybody in the world could feel," Krenzel said, "with that kind of excitement, that natural high."

- -

Hear the Victory Bell Ring (or Try Not to)

For 60 years, that same lifeless tone has blared across campus after each Ohio State victory. Ohio Stadium's Victory Bell clangs for 15 minutes following each triumph and the steady, plodding note can ring in one's ears for hours after the fact.

After each home football victory, the Victory Bell rings for 15 minutes.

Iris S. and Bert L. Wolst...
FOOTBALL CENTER

The graduating classes of 1943, 1944, and 1954 joined forces to contribute the bulky apparatus to the university. The bell, which weighs 2,420 pounds, hangs in the southeast tower of the stadium, 150 feet from the ground. The bell cost $2,535 to install. On a tranquil Saturday afternoon, the sound waves can travel several miles. Though more than 100,000 fans pack The Horseshoe to capacity and thousands more watch on TV at home or at the bar, anyone in the area who failed to catch the game can learn Ohio State's fate by whether he or she hears the 15 minutes of ringing.

After Woody Hayes' Buckeyes dispatched California 21–13 on October 2, 1954, members of the organization Alpha Phi Omega took turns at tugging at the strings to initiate the bell's swaying motion, which elicits the loud chime. Since the contraption is so stout, the person tasked with jerking it can occasionally be lifted off of their feet.

The evening before Ohio State's affair with Iowa in November 1965, someone stole the bell's clapper—the pendulum that hangs from the bell and swings from side to side. The clapper stands three feet tall and weighs about 60 pounds. It was discovered five days later, on the statue of former university president William Oxley Thompson that resided on The Oval. With it was a note that read:

Here is the clapper
That rings the bell
That hangs in the tower
That's part of the Stadium
That belongs to Woody

For the first quarter-century of the bell's existence, Hayes directed the Buckeyes to victories that prompted the mechanism's deafening toll. It drowns out the postgame conversation as students retreat to their residences, fans head back to their cars, reporters seek answers from the coach, and players apply ice to their aching limbs.

The bell rings for only 15 minutes, but it seems like hours. After a victory over rival Michigan, the students will tug at the bell for 30 minutes, signifying the extra-sweet triumph. As Ivan Pavlov learned with his dog, a repeated action eventually extorts a patterned response. Even those not within earshot of campus can probably hear a mental chime after an Ohio State win. For those who have heard it live, it is difficult to forget that same dull note over and over again.

. . . .

Full Circle

The Big Ten is slow. The Big Ten does not have SEC speed. The Big Ten is a weak, inferior, archaic conference. The style of play, with a big, bruising running back, a beefy offensive line, and an in-the-pocket game manager at quarterback, is antiquated. The conference is dying.

The genesis for those perspectives originated with the 2007 BCS Championship Game. The 2008 BCS Championship Game pushed that agenda forward another few steps. Ohio State was there when the narrative began, responsible for it to an extent. The Buckeyes were also there when it ended. Everything came full circle and Ohio State seemed to always be in the middle of it all.

Jim Tressel's Buckeyes stormed their way to the BCS Championship Game in 2006. They pushed aside their opponents and, when No. 2 Michigan visited Ohio Stadium in the final week of the regular season, they emerged victorious. They looked fast. They looked aggressive. They looked unstoppable. Against other Big Ten teams, of course. They did topple No. 2 Texas in early September, though. So when the Buckeyes arrived in Arizona for a Fiesta Bowl matchup with Florida, they were designated heavy favorites. The Gators then thrashed Ohio State.

Ted Ginn Jr. returned the opening kick for a touchdown. The Buckeyes seemed poised to win by 70. Not so fast.

"I think that was the changer. Everybody, you are jacked up, you come out like a bunch of caged animals and then, bam," said Florida coach Urban Meyer. "We are all on [our] heels and the offense systematically goes down and converted three or four first downs and everybody settled down and said 'Let's go play.'

"If we punted there, they go down again and score—which obviously they have the weapons to do that—you are in a storm. What was the turning point of the game? The first drive by the offense."

Ohio State lost by 27. Urban Meyer's group looked fast. It looked aggressive. It looked unstoppable. Against a Big Ten team, of course.

"They looked fast on film and they proved to be as fast as they looked on film," said Ohio State offensive lineman Doug Datish.

Beyond the 41–14 final score sat a slew of shocking statistics. Ohio State gained 82 total yards on 37 plays, an average of 2.2 yards per snap. Heisman Trophy–winning quarterback Troy Smith completed four of 14 passes for 35 yards. Brian Hartline led Ohio State receivers with 13 yards. The Buckeyes recorded eight first downs, two of which resulted from Florida penalties.

Florida's Derrick Harvey registered three sacks. Jarvis Moss tallied two. They made life difficult for Smith.

"He was rattled, running for his life," Harvey said. "That's what good 'D' made him do."

Tressel surmised that Ohio State's effort against Michigan in November—a 42–39 triumph—exhausted his team and left it ill-equipped for the demands of a national title bout.

"Our '06 team had been undefeated and had really emptied their emotional gas tank a month before with the Ohio State–Michigan game and No. 1 versus No. 2 and all that stuff," Tressel said. "You could see it was a little bit difficult, as hard as we tried to be at that same level as we were that day in late November."

Tressel said the Buckeyes "just didn't get the job done across the board. We always talk about [how] you get as your works deserve, and we didn't deserve to be champions."

A dominant regular season, a pair of wins as the No. 1 team in the nation against the No. 2 team—all of it was overshadowed by a harrowing, lopsided defeat on the grandest stage against a hungry, motivated underdog. The Gators embraced that role. Meyer saturated his players' brains with the concept. Everyone thought Ohio State was the superior team. Everyone thought Florida was there just because the Buckeyes had to play someone, and preferably not Michigan for the second time. No one thought the game would be close. No one thought Florida actually deserved to spend a week in Arizona. Some of that was true. Meyer, though, pounded each theory into his players' heads.

"We use that quite a bit," Meyer said. "And I'm guilty of that. But then our players, it was like a feeding frenzy. Once we started seeing how it was, [it was] sharks in the water once that thing got going."

Florida entered halftime with a 34–14 advantage. A typical intermission involves the players taking a seat and getting hydrated, trainers making the rounds and preparing everyone for the final 30 minutes, and coaches discussing what adjustments need to take place. Such a scene would make sense for a team boasting a 20-point lead. Meyer, however, walked into the locker room and saw a group of players, helmets still on, pounding away at the lockers and rallying together.

"It was a feeding frenzy that was going on in that locker room," Meyer said. "What do you attribute that to? Chance to win a national championship? Absolutely. Chance to play a great football team and let the country see you have some good players, too."

Someone had given Meyer a book that chronicled Ohio State's "2006 championship season," as the cover of the paperback proclaims. The book was published prior to the BCS Championship Game. It detailed how the Buckeyes marched to a 12–0 record. According to the coach, the Gators accounted for only two pages in the entire text. Meyer said the Florida staff spent 45 minutes of a team meeting one day during bowl game preparation discussing the book.

"When you are dealing with 18- to 21-year-olds, any little stoke you can give them, we are going to give them," Meyer said. "As a coach, you try to watch the response. You try to go certain ways with a team. If you don't get the response, stop it and go another way."

The coaches got the response for which they were looking. Ohio State had 51 days between its regular season–capping victory against Michigan and the national title game. For the first two weeks, media types prattled on about who was worthy of being Ohio State's final victim. Did USC deserve a shot? Would Florida warrant consideration? Should Michigan merit a rematch?

Once USC lost to UCLA and Florida was selected to square off against Ohio State, the final five weeks of buildup were dedicated to highlighting the supposed disparity in talent between the Buckeyes and Gators. Meyer basked in the disrespect.

"We as a staff felt, and the seniors felt, that was going to be the M.O. for the game: 'Let's show them we have good players, too,'" Meyer said. "The media blitz that went on for 30 days certainly was advantageous for the Gators. The human element takes over, you get patted on the back so many times, you actually believe you are pretty good."

But were the Gators actually long shots, or was this the beginning of a college football cycle, one that would see the SEC take command of the sport? The Buckeyes did not stroll into the title game the following year as they had in 2006. They were ranked No. 1 again for four weeks in October and November, but they fell short against Illinois at The Horseshoe. A series of late-season losses by top-ranked teams still propelled Ohio State into a second consecutive BCS Championship Game as the No. 1 team. This time, the Buckeyes faced a different SEC team: LSU.

Immediately, talk centered on Ohio State's reputation and how the program would be judged if it dropped a second straight title game against a southern foe. Tressel said the team used the Florida loss for instructional and motivational gains.

"What's most important is how you feel about yourself and where it is as a part of who you are," he said the day before the championship battle. "And so the biggest goal we have is to play as good as we can possibly play and us coming close or perhaps even doing that will really help us paint ourselves in a good light, regardless of what the outcome is. If we don't play as well as we're capable of playing, we'll paint ourselves not in as good a light as we would like because we knew we were capable of more.

"If you worry about much more than that, then I think you have things out of perspective."

Just like the year before, the Buckeyes sprinted out to a blistering start. Beanie Wells dashed 65 yards to the end zone on Ohio State's opening drive. After forcing LSU into a quick punt, the Buckeyes tacked on a field goal for a 10–0 edge. The Tigers rattled off the next 31 points. LSU captured the crystal football with a 38–24 win.

"It hurt tremendously," Wells said. "I mean, the pain, you really can't compare it to anything. To go to the national championship twice and lose, I mean, it's incredible."

Ohio State fared better against LSU than it did against Florida, but consecutive championship game losses spoke louder than any moral victory. The Buckeyes actually outgained the Tigers in total yardage, but they also committed more penalties and more turnovers. The SEC notched its second straight national title triumph. Ohio State was reeling. The Buckeyes were easy targets for scrutiny. Tressel's bunch dropped the ball for two straight years after a pair of commendable regular seasons. Would anyone elect to see the Buckeyes on the grand stage again if they were in contention for a third straight BCS Championship Game appearance? How could voters take Ohio State seriously?

"I don't worry too much about criticism because if you're not tough enough to handle criticism," Tressel said, "then you better get out of this game, because there are a whole lot of people that have interest in this game. And there are a whole lot of people that don't really have much understanding of what it takes to be good at this game but yet love to have opinions. If you struggle taking criticism, then you need to not be at Ohio State or not be playing the game of football."

Meyer and the Gators emerged triumphant in the title game again in 2008. The Buckeyes fell short against Texas in the Fiesta Bowl. Alabama continued the SEC's tradition in 2009 and Auburn carried the torch in 2010. Nick Saban's Crimson Tide squad rolled over fellow SEC member LSU in the 2011 title game and throttled Notre Dame on the grand stage a year later. All told, the SEC claimed seven straight national championships until Florida State eclipsed Auburn in the 2013 affair. Meanwhile, Michigan and Penn State, two traditional Big Ten powers, were down. Ohio State had won only one bowl game— the Rose Bowl following the 2009 campaign—during that stretch, two if including the since-vacated Sugar Bowl against Arkansas after the 2010 season. Perception of the conferences could not have been more different.

Then, Meyer, the man whose Gators team started the SEC's string of dominance, swiftly put an end to it. He directed Ohio State to a 42–35 victory against Alabama, a game in which the Buckeyes proved they had plenty of speed and athleticism and talent. Ezekiel Elliott sprinted past the Crimson Tide defense en route to 230 yards. The SEC school involved was not the only one with four- and five-star recruits. The SEC school proved not to have Big Ten speed. No longer did representing the highly regarded conference mean a cakewalk to the championship game.

Michigan State had defeated Baylor in the Cotton Bowl. Wisconsin had dispatched Auburn in the Outback Bowl. Ohio State's besting of Alabama capped a much-needed season of salvation for the Big Ten.

"There's a perception out there that we're not [on the same level as the SEC]," Meyer said. "There's a perception out here. I'll tell you when I think the tide turned a little bit was when Wisconsin beat Auburn. Everybody on our team knew that. I made sure they knew that. [And] when Michigan State came back and beat an excellent Baylor team. And maybe the Big Ten is not that bad. Maybe the Big Ten is pretty damn good. And it's certainly getting better.

"You've been told you've been bad for so long, at times the psychologist part of it takes over. You start believing you're not very good, and that's not true at all. The same thing with the quality of football. High school football players in the North and the Midwest, they're great. Is the quantity a little bit lesser? Sure, the quantity is, but not the quality. The quality is outstanding, and I think that was a testimony of what happened in that game."

The Buckeyes had fallen behind the Crimson Tide 21–6 in the first half of the Sugar Bowl. At that point, Meyer had to rely on what he had preached to his players all week. A few days before the bowl game, the team had a guest speaker talk about how unwavering faith can increase a group's level of play. The contrary can also prove true, the speaker contended. Meyer repeated that mantra at the team's pregame meal and again while the team watched a short highlight video prior to boarding the bus to the stadium. When the Buckeyes watched Wisconsin—a team they had shellacked 59–0 in the Big Ten Championship Game—outlast SEC adversary Auburn in overtime, that served as a turning point. Meyer called it "a major, major moment for us getting ready for this game." Then, the Spartans finished off an improbable comeback. The tides were shifting. The Big Ten was on its way back. Ohio State would be the final nail in the coffin.

"You should have seen their faces," Meyer said. "They knew. They knew."

The Buckeyes simply needed to believe.

"The mind is a fragile thing," Meyer said. "You know, all of a sudden you get down against a team like that, that's No. 1 in recruiting every year for the past six, seven years, our guys know that. You see them on film. Great team. But we're pretty good, too. And we go in East Lansing and beat a team that beat Baylor [and] to play the way we did against Wisconsin, a team that just beat Auburn, that's the psychological approach to getting 18-, 19-, 20-year-olds to believe."

After what Meyer termed a "breakthrough" win, the Buckeyes advanced to Arlington, Texas, where they defeated the Oregon Ducks 42–20 to shoo away the ghosts of failed title games past, vindicate the Big Ten from another year of criticism, and silence the SEC backers who deemed, for nearly a decade, every other conference greatly inferior. After nine years, everything came full circle.

"There's one way to silence people and that's go out and play," Meyer said. "At some point you're going to get good results and I'm very fired up for our conference right now, because at some point it gets exhausting when you keep hearing and hearing and then you start believing."

· ·

Visit the Oval

O ne day, it is a winter wonderland, a picturesque representation of the serenity and beauty that often accompanies the harsh, unrelenting grip of the calendar's coldest months. Another day, it plays host to a sandless beach. It is a grassy domain overflowing with scantily clad 20-somethings who have waited months for the sun to peek out from behind the seemingly permanent clouds and for the mercury in the thermometer to nudge past freezing temperatures.

When the snow melts, students, faculty, and passersby occupy The Oval in the center of campus to read, play catch, walk a dog, or relax.

The Oval is the epicenter of Ohio State's campus. It is, in fact, an oval. It does, in fact, reside in the center of campus. It is an 11-acre beacon of green space left open to the whims of anyone who chooses to occupy it.

The original design for Ohio State's campus did not include an Oval or anything resembling a large, open space. That changed in 1893, when the master design plan proposed a cluster of buildings surrounding a central opening. In 1910, that opening was first referred to as "The Oval."

When Mother Nature permits during the spring and summer months, The Oval attracts visitors from all walks of life. Students throw around a football or a Frisbee. Workers on lunch breaks eat their meals, read books, or skim through their phones while sitting on a bench or up against a tree, where they can benefit from some shade. Bikini-clad women lie on towels in the grass and soak up the sun. People walk their dogs. Students rushing to class whiz by on one of the many pathways that intersect the area. Others merely stroll the cement passages and soak up the scene.

During the winter months, the vast land is largely uninhabited, save for the occasional class-goer. The setting is alluring, with snow lining the trees and smothering the grass. Its role as the center of the action, however, goes into hibernation. Then, as the wintry precipitation melts away and spring blossoms, the first 50-degree day of the year will bait students into transforming the area back into a grassy beach.

. . . .

Third (String) and Long

Urban Meyer sat before a microphone, sporting a black Nike T-shirt that declared his team the victor in the Sugar Bowl. Ohio State had just wrapped up a thrilling, albeit exhausting, win against Alabama. An upset, unquestionably. In a week and a half, the Buckeyes would square off against Oregon for the national championship. During the press conference following the Sugar Bowl, a reporter asked a question that casually mentioned that Oregon won its semifinal game against Florida State earlier in the day by 39 points. Meyer, eyebrows raised, interjected.

"Oregon won by 40?" he said, seemingly in a state of disbelief.

"What was it, 59 to 20?" the reporter said.

"Oh," Meyer said with a smirk. "I gotta go. We gotta go get ready for that one."

Meyer jokingly started to get up to leave, headed for the film room. He sat back in his seat, a smile on his face. Who would have thought that after the first of the year, the Buckeyes would have to prepare for anything other than the bone-chilling temperatures Mother Nature bestows upon the Midwest each winter? A season-ending injury to quarterback Braxton Miller figured to eliminate any chance at national glory. A Week 2 loss at home to Virginia Tech hammered that concept home. J.T. Barrett, a relatively unknown commodity at the start of the season, performed admirably, but even he was lost for the year in late November.

A third-string quarterback. The shocking death of a player. A semifinal opponent many assumed was destined for another title. The odds were certainly stacked against Meyer's bunch in 2014. Oregon's assault on Florida State only served as another hurdle. The 59–20 Rose Bowl result would not deter a team that had surmounted plenty of daunting tasks through the duration of the season. For months, the Buckeyes were facing third-and-long. Every time, they converted. On January 12, they converted their final tall order into the program's eighth national championship.

"I've been asked a lot, 'Did I see this happening?'" Meyer said. "I saw a team that prepared very well."

Braxton Miller initially injured his shoulder during the 2014 Orange Bowl. The quarterback said he played through pain—after taking a hit on the opening drive against Clemson—that registered at a "9.5" on a scale of 1-10. He had surgery a month later. While making a basic pass during practice in August, he reinjured the shoulder and needed a second operation. The second surgery ended his 2014 season before it even began.

Enter Barrett, a 19-year-old Texas kid who had never thrown a collegiate pass. Miller had amassed more than 5,000 passing yards and 3,000 rushing yards in his three seasons on the field for the Buckeyes. He had tallied 84 touchdowns altogether, one shy of Art Schlichter's school record and sixth all-time in the Big Ten. He

EXTRA POINTS

Barrett's Blossoming

Altogether, Ohio State established or tied 74 season or game records during the 2014 campaign. They set 26 team records, including tying the NCAA mark for wins in a season. They shattered the conference records for offensive yards and first downs in a season and program records for points scored and passes completed. A handful of players accounted for individual marks in the history books as well, including redshirt freshman quarterback J.T. Barrett, who set 19 program records. The man who finished fifth in balloting for the Heisman Trophy missed the team's final three games. Here is a list of Barrett's feats.

Touchdowns responsible for in a season: 45 (also a Big Ten record)

Freshman of the Week awards in a season: 7 (also a Big Ten record)

Touchdown passes in a season: 34

Total yards in a season: 3,772

Career completion percentage: 64.6 percent

Touchdown passes in a game: 6

Touchdowns responsible for in a game: 6

Career passing yards per game: 236.2

Consecutive passes completed in a season: 12

Passing efficiency for a season: 169.8

Most wins by a first-year starting quarterback: 11 (tied with Todd Boeckman)

Average total offensive yards for a season: 314.3

Average total offensive yards for a career: 314.3

Games gaining 200 or more yards of total offense in a season: 11

Games gaining 300 or more yards of total offense in a season: 7

Games gaining 400 or more yards of total offense in a season: 1

Rushing yards by a quarterback in a game: 189

Longest rush by a quarterback: 86 yards

had also racked up 26 wins as Ohio State's starting quarterback. Barrett, who redshirted as a freshman, had never even been under consideration to play in a game. He wrestled away the backup quarterback position from Cardale Jones during summer practice. Once Miller was ruled out for the season, Barrett took over and took off.

He struggled against Virginia Tech. The Buckeyes beat Navy in their opener, but the Hokies presented problems. Barrett completed only nine of 29 passes and he tossed three interceptions. A late pick-six sealed Virginia Tech's triumph. Barrett had little issue from there on, though. A week after the defeat—one that led talking heads to proclaim that Ohio State had removed itself from any potential College Football Playoff consideration—Barrett tied a program record with six touchdowns in a blowout win against Kent State. Over the next three weeks, he totaled 14 touchdowns, three of which came via his legs.

Ohio State's offense, under the direction of coordinator Tom Herman, was rolling. But a game under the lights against Penn State at Beaver Stadium proved challenging. A Nittany Lions field goal with nine seconds remaining advanced the game into overtime. A hobbled Barrett, however, rushed for a game-tying touchdown in the first extra period and another to commence the second. Joey Bosa, a relentless savage on Ohio State's defensive line, shoved a Penn State offensive lineman into quarterback Christian Hackenberg for a self-inflicted, contest-ending, fourth-down sack. The Buckeyes maintained their unblemished conference record.

"The first overtime against Penn State was in my opinion the turning point, when I saw a team that didn't play very well," Meyer said. "I don't want to say anything against Penn State because Penn State has got a fine team. But the script was written. We should have lost that game. It happens every year where a team loses a league [game], doesn't play very good. Every excuse in the world to lose that game, a quarterback playing on a sprained MCL, freshmen that didn't play very well—and they found a way to win that game. That's when I personally walked in the locker room after, going, 'That could have been a program changer for us.'"

The Buckeyes arrived in East Lansing, Michigan, on November 8 with a 7–1 mark, including 4–0 in Big Ten play. Michigan State, the team that crushed Ohio State's national title dreams 11 months earlier, entered the affair with a 7–1 record and the No. 7 ranking. Meyer's squad got vengeance. Barrett accounted for 386 total yards. Running back Ezekiel Elliott gained 154 on the ground. The Buckeyes crossed into the end zone seven times in a 49–37 victory. They fended off Minnesota and Indiana and were en route to the same fate against Michigan in the final week of the regular season when Barrett's ankle snapped on a running play. Jones finished out the 42–28 win and the Buckeyes earned a berth in the conference title game, but with little in the way of momentum. How could a team employing its third-string quarterback solve a stingy Wisconsin defense? Could Ohio State stall Badgers running back Melvin Gordon, a Heisman Trophy finalist and the nation's leading rusher?

Even if Ohio State were to prevail, the Buckeyes seemed to be on the outside looking in when it came to the College Football Playoff committee rankings. They were ranked No. 5. The top four advanced to the playoff. And would the committee evaluate the team based on its performance with Jones under center, rather than what the team accomplished with Barrett, a Heisman Trophy finalist, as its signal-caller?

Meyer lauded Jones' ability, despite the fact that the Cleveland native had never started a collegiate game. The coach noted how the quarterback "is a product of those around him," though he admitted Jones would have to make plays for the Buckeyes to emerge victorious. He said Jones had a "very good touch" and was "a very good passer." Jones actually held the lead on Barrett during spring practice in the battle for the backup quarterback position, but Barrett overtook his teammate by excelling with intangibles, such as identifying the weakness of the defense and its coverage scheme, providing leadership, and properly assembling the offensive unit.

Meyer felt better about Jones' potential in those regards once he became the team's starter in December.

"I feel he's much more prepared in that area," Meyer said. "So much of quarterbacking is not just throwing the ball, but why you're throwing it there, the protection issues, just the complete saturation that a quarterback must have to run an offense. The throwing the ball part is probably 10 percent. If you're not a quarterback at this level, you can't throw the ball. It's getting to the point of where the ball goes, all the complications that you have to do before, the protection. Most quarterbacks you see struggle, it's not because they can't throw. It's because of the understanding of where you're going with the ball, how to make sure you're protected."

The Buckeyes' psyche took another blow well before kickoff, though. Defensive lineman Kosta Karageorge, a walk-on, was found dead of an apparent self-inflicted gunshot wound the day after the Michigan game. He had been missing for four days.

"We're trained to handle adverse situations, but obviously not something of this magnitude," said offensive tackle Taylor Decker. "We're trained to play football and this is so much more than that. Football is just a game and people blow it out of proportion and make it a lot bigger than it is. We just have to go back to each other, lean on each other for strength because obviously it's hard for a lot of people."

Just three days before the Big Ten Championship Game, many players attended the funeral for their teammate.

"I don't think he'd want for anything like this to hold us back," Decker said. "He was a huge team guy."

And so the Buckeyes forged ahead. They returned to a familiar scene, too. They arrived at Lucas Oil Stadium in Indianapolis, the site where they fell short in the same game a year earlier. In that instance, Michigan State derailed the Buckeyes' chances at facing Florida State for the crystal football. Meyer had not wiped the memory from his mental hard drive.

THE CATCH

The Buckeyes have had Oregon's number in recent years.

Tight ends have never been the most involved receivers in Ohio State's passing game. So when the Buckeyes faced a third down and needed 13 yards to keep Oregon's high-octane offense off the field during the 2010 Rose Bowl, no one could have anticipated it would be tight end Jake Ballard coming away with a reception marked by athleticism and timing.

The Buckeyes, who had lost each of their last three bowl games—all BCS bowl games, for that matter—clutched a two-point lead with nine minutes remaining. Quarterback Terrelle Pryor took the snap out of a shotgun formation, drifted backward, and scrambled to his right in an attempt to evade a pair of Oregon rushers. Pryor slung the ball 25 yards downfield, essentially up for grabs. Ballard twisted his body back toward the line of scrimmage, leapt in the air above a flock of Ducks defenders, extended both hands high above his head, and hauled in the pass.

"I jumped and I thought I jumped too early," said the six-foot, six-inch Ballard. "Then I kept going up. So maybe the adrenaline helped me get a couple more inches."

The conversion placed the ball at the Oregon 31-yard line, setting up the Buckeyes for the game-clinching score when Pryor connected with receiver DeVier Posey for a 17-yard touchdown just five plays later. The Buckeyes left Pasadena, California, with a 26–17 win.

"I didn't think anything else except, 'I have to make this catch,'" Ballard said. "'There is no other choice.'"

"That was a tough day, walking off that field," he said, reminiscing about Ohio State's 34–24 loss. "Obviously, we played a very good team and came up short. Great game. Down 17 points. Come back, take a lead. Back and forth, back and forth. Came down to a few critical plays. I haven't spent a whole lot of time, but for me to say I didn't think about that moment when I walked in that place, I did."

The team held a prayer and a moment of silence for Karageorge and his family prior to taking the field before kickoff. Players wore decals with his No. 53 on the back of their helmets and fellow defensive lineman Michael Bennett changed his jersey number to No. 53.

Jake Ballard's leaping catch in the 2010 Rose Bowl helped secure Ohio State's victory against Oregon.

"We'll never forget our teammate," Meyer said.

He would have been proud. Two minutes into the contest, Jones connected with receiver Devin Smith on a 39-yard touchdown, a throw over the top of the defense that turned heads and rid the quarterback of any first-start jitters. No need for nerves when life's a breeze. The Buckeyes steamrolled the Badgers. They outgained Wisconsin by 300 yards. They averaged 10 yards per play. They forced four turnovers. Elliott gained 220 yards on 20 carries. Gordon was limited to 76 on 26 totes. Ohio State won 59–0. A statement victory, no doubt. Let the politicking commence.

"This is without question the most improved team from start to finish that I've ever been around," Meyer said after Ohio State's rout, Wisconsin's first shutout loss in 17 years. "To see them operate in all facets of the game at a high, high level from our punter to the way we played defense, then offense was incredible. Our third quarterback, two Heisman candidates out, this guy comes in and plays like that.

"The Selection Committee has a tough job. The whole BCS thing, this is supposed to clean up the BCS conflict or conversations. All I can speak to is I've been around teams that have competed and won national championships. This team, the way it's playing right now, is one of the top teams in America."

In the face of adversity, the Buckeyes persevered.

"These are great guys that come together," Meyer said. "In a tough week, a close team got even closer."

It helped that the team spent what Meyer termed "an inordinate amount of time" on leadership training. The coaching staff endured a five-week program in the spring. Meyer emphasized a theme of the team being a "brotherhood of trust." The staff preached the importance of understanding "E+R=O," which stands for event plus response equals outcome. In the end, it allowed the group to persevere through adverse elements in what developed into a trying, yet rewarding, season, one that culminated in being selected as the No. 4 seed for the first edition of the College Football Playoff.

"It was mind-blowing," Jones said, "because thinking back to September or late August, everybody counted us out. It was just a shocker."

Not to Meyer, it was not.

"You really have to be selfless to be good," Meyer said. "Now that I'm a little older, been around some really good teams, the closeness in the locker room, how they care for each other, to be able to fight through adversity, that's easy to measure.

"Football is one sport that exposes you quicker than I think any sport there is. If you're a selfish player, you get exposed. If you are not working, you get exposed. That's why my comment about this team—this team has been through a lot. They keep grinding and they keep winning."

Maybe Alabama's early 21–6 lead in the Sugar Bowl meant the Buckeyes had reached the end of their leash. Maybe it indicated that a team on its third quarterback, a team that had suffered so much emotional anguish, could only venture so far.

Maybe not.

Ohio State narrowed its deficit to 21–13 before deploying some trickery in the waning moments of the first half. With 19 seconds left and the ball on Alabama's 13-yard line, Jones stood in the shotgun with Elliott to his right. Jalin Marshall, lined up in the slot, motioned over and took a handoff from Jones. He then flipped the ball to receiver Evan Spencer, who ran toward the backfield. Spencer stopped, gripped the football, and lofted a pass to the front left corner of the end zone, just above the reach of cornerback Cyrus Jones and into the welcoming hands of receiver Michael Thomas, who planted his left foot just inside the white out-of-bounds line.

"I knew when it would get called, I'd have a great chance of making it happen," Spencer said. "Once I saw it was looking like a good look that we needed, I was just licking my chops and I let it go and hoped that he could go get the ball and get his feet in bounds."

Spencer engaged in a celebratory high-step to the sideline. Thomas bounced back up and skipped around the end zone. The Buckeyes were back in it and they would receive to start the second half.

"Lou Holtz used to always say this, when I worked for him, when he first hired me at Notre Dame in 1996, he said: 'The momentum, especially for a young team, is worth at least seven to 14 points during the course of a game. And the most important momentum of any game is the last five minutes of the first half, first five minutes of the second half.' We came out smoking in the second half, too, because I could hear it as we were walking in: 'We get the ball. We get the ball.'"

Smith hauled in a 47-yard touchdown from Jones to open the second stanza. Defensive end Steve Miller took the football and ran, scoring on a 41-yard interception return as the Buckeyes roared back with 28 unanswered points. Elliott's 85-yard sprint to the end zone with three minutes remaining gave Ohio State a 42–28 lead. The Crimson Tide closed to within 42–35 and had one last, faint shot at a game-tying touchdown, but safety Tyvis Powell picked off Blake Sims as the clock struck zero on Alabama.

Time to prepare for Oregon.

The quarterback comparison for the national championship game was fascinating. The Ducks boasted the Heisman Trophy winner, a man in Marcus Mariota who concluded his collegiate career with 136 total touchdowns and only 14 interceptions in three years as a starter. Jones had started only two games, both at neutral sites against top competition.

Ohio State made Mariota appear human. He threw for 333 yards, but much of it was in an attempt to rally his side back from a sizable deficit. The Buckeyes grabbed a first-quarter advantage and did not relinquish it. Elliott iced the game with a trio of rushing touchdowns in the final 15 minutes, as he amassed 246 yards on the ground and four touchdowns. The Buckeyes captured their first national title since 2002, but this game did not require a pair of overtimes, much-ballyhooed penalty flags, or a knee injury to a gifted running back. There was no fourth-quarter nail-biting. Ohio State systematically dismantled Oregon en route to a convincing 42–20 win. Oregon won by 39 in its semifinal matchup. The Buckeyes beat Oregon by 22. They did it with their third choice at quarterback. They did it four months after a sobering home nonconference loss. They did it after grieving through the death of a teammate.

Much of that speaks to the effort of Meyer and his coaching staff. Ohio State football historian Jack Park called it "maybe the greatest coaching job" in program lore.

"He held that team together," Park said.

Not even Meyer could have envisioned that.

"This team wasn't supposed to do this," Meyer said, "but they fought through adversity, they got stronger and stronger and stronger, and this is a great team. We finished the year a great team. To have four turnovers and still beat a team like that 42–20—incredible experience. I don't want to get over dramatic, but it's as improved a football team—and I've watched football for a long time—from Game 1 to Game 15. I've never seen anything like it.

"To say we had this vision back in September or even August, no, not a chance."

Championship Pedigree

O hio State is credited with eight national championships. All are recognized by the NCAA, but only five of them include AP No. 1 rankings, typically regarded as the voice of reason in a world long without a system in place to decide upon a consensus champion. Each title was earned with hard work, perseverance, and all of the other superlatives that coaches love to deploy when commending their players. The truth is the Buckeyes have won each championship in a different fashion.

Urban Meyer's 2014 squad played 15 games, including two playoff tilts. The Buckeyes amassed a 14–1 record, including wins in the Big Ten Championship Game and the Sugar Bowl and a victory in the College Football Playoff Championship on January 12. Woody Hayes' 1961 group played only nine games. The Buckeyes emerged victorious in eight of them, as they finished a season-opening affair with TCU engaged in a 7–7 deadlock. There was no football playoff, no BCS computer system, no algorithm for determining an undisputed national champion. Ohio State beat Michigan on November 25 and its season was over. Ohio State's faculty council opted against the football team playing in the Rose Bowl, so the Buckeyes finished with an 8–0–1 record, which proved worthy enough to be awarded the distinction of national champions by the Football Writers Association of America.

Woody's teams collected five national championships during his 28-year tenure in Columbus. All five included unbeaten Big Ten records and all but the 1961 campaign ended in a trip to Pasadena, California, for the Rose Bowl. Following the 1954, 1957, and 1968 seasons, Ohio State emerged triumphant on New Year's Day to capture the national crown. In 1970, the 9–0 Buckeyes lost to Stanford 27–17, but they had been awarded the title of national champions by the National Football Foundation prior to their trek out west.

Paul Brown's 1942 team finished with the No. 1 ranking after a 9–1 season, which earned the program its first national title. Woody's bunch in 1954 racked up 10 wins, including a Rose Bowl victory against USC, en route to an undefeated national championship season. Three years later, the Buckeyes recovered from a season-opening home loss to TCU to finish 9–1, including a 7–0 mark in conference play. After a 10–7 win against Oregon in the Rose Bowl, the Buckeyes finished No. 1 in the coaches' poll, No. 2 in the AP poll, and No. 1 in the FWAA poll.

There was no disputing Ohio State's merits in 1968. The "Super Sophomores," a gifted second-year class led by quarterback Rex Kern, running back Jim Otis, and safety Jack Tatum, plowed through the opposition. A 27–16 win in the Rose Bowl over USC gave the Buckeyes a 10–0 record that included a 13–0 win against No. 1 Purdue and a 50–14 shellacking against No. 4 Michigan. That group appeared destined for a repeat in 1969, as the Buckeyes demolished their opponents until falling flat at Michigan in their final game, a defeat that cost Ohio State a chance at another championship. In 1970, the senior-laden team squashed Michigan to enter the Rose Bowl with an unbeaten record.

The Buckeyes then went more than 30 years without a national title. Jim Tressel ended the drought when he held the crystal football trophy above his head on January 3, 2003. Tressel's 2002 team— the second he coached in Columbus—became the first group in the history of college football to finish a season 14–0. Over time, both nonconference and conference schedules grew in number of games. The Buckeyes nearly slipped up a handful of times, but a double-overtime upset of top-ranked Miami in the BCS Championship Game solidified their status atop the college football ranks.

Under Tressel's guidance, Ohio State had its chances to add to the trophy case, but the Buckeyes fell short in consecutive years against

Florida and LSU. Not until Meyer directed Ohio State and third-string quarterback Cardale Jones to the four-team playoff in 2014 did the Buckeyes return to prominence. No longer, though, can a team simply rack up nine or 10 wins and garner all of the accolades. A 10-win season in Columbus is now considered a dire disappointment. Of course, as of 2014, only one national champion can be honored, a result of the College Football Playoff system instituted to avoid having to rely on computer formulas to determine the two teams most deserving of competing in the title game. Ohio State entered the inaugural playoff as the No. 4 seed, but the Buckeyes upset No. 1 Alabama in New Orleans and No. 2 Oregon in Dallas to clinch the eighth championship in school history.

See Script Ohio Performed

The marching band sprawled out across the grass at Ohio Stadium in 1932 and, for the first time, spelled out the word *Ohio.*

Only, that was the University of Michigan's marching band. And it is not, as longtime members and supporters of Ohio State's band will attest, the first rendition of the ritual that the Buckeyes have performed since 1936. Four years later, on October 10, 1936, during halftime of Ohio State's affair against Pittsburgh, the Buckeyes' Marching Band executed its first arrangement of Script Ohio. Under the guidance of band director Eugene J. Weigel, the band grouped into a triple Block O formation and then uncoiled to spell out the script letters in the state's name. As a drum major captains the movement around the outside of the letters, every band member

The Ohio State Marching Band performs the marvel known as Script Ohio at each home football game.

remains in motion. All the while, the band played the tune of Le Régiment de Sambre et Meuse, a French military march.

A fourth- or fifth-year sousaphone player is traditionally selected to "dot the 'I'." Originally, this was no special honor. John Brungart, an E-flat cornet player, was the first to complete the action. He returned to dot the "I" in 1986 to commemorate the 50th anniversary of the tradition.

In 1937, drum major Myron McKelvey prematurely arrived at his post atop the "I", so sousaphone player Glen Johnson turned and bowed to the crowd to kill time. McKelvey finished three or four measures too

HONORARY DOTTERS

Woody Hayes did not play the sousaphone. The legendary football coach is, however, one of a handful of honorary dignitaries to dot the I in the marching band's performance of Script Ohio.

A sousaphone player must give up his or her opportunity to dot the I for an honorary selection to execute the long-standing tradition. Here is a list of honorary dotters:

1971: University president Novice Fawcett and his wife
1978: Comedian Bob Hope
1983: Woody Hayes
1985: University ticket director Robert Ries
1990: World heavyweight champion James "Buster" Douglas (seven months earlier, he defeated Mike Tyson in a world-renowned upset)
1995: University president Gordon Gee and his wife
2003: All 13 seniors on the 2002 national champion football team (took place at the championship celebration at The Horseshoe on January 19, 2003)
2006: Golfer Jack Nicklaus
2009: Senator and astronaut John Glenn and his wife
2011: CEO of The Limited Brands Les Wexner
2011: Ohio State Marching Band director Jon Woods

Longtime marching band directors Paul Droste and Jack Evans and composer Dick Heine are also said to have dotted the I. It is an honor very few alumni ever receive.

"It's the one position, as I get older, that I think I may trade being the starting quarterback at Ohio State for," said former quarterback Bill Long. "That band is so good. They practiced as hard as we did. When you're down there low, watching them—it's impossible, what they did. The Script Ohio, it's impossible."

soon, so, as Johnson once explained, he "did a big kick, a turn and a deep bow to use up the music." The crowd erupted in a cheer. The bow and high leg strut have been woven into the fabric of the band's signature performance.

The drum major leading the charge high fives the person dotting the "I" toward the end of the formation. They then saunter over to the top of the incomplete letter and the drum major points to the spot of the dot, as the dotter turns and bows to both sides of the stadium before occupying the empty space.

On occasion, the marching band will add some members and execute a double Script Ohio, first performed in 1966 at a game between Ohio State and Texas Christian University. Ohio State has also welcomed members of its alumni marching band to The Horseshoe. The hundreds of musicians have joined forces to complete a quadruple Script Ohio, with one version facing each of the four sides of the stadium. This was first displayed in 1977, at a contest between Ohio State and the University of Miami. In September 2013, Ohio Stadium hosted 21 students from the Ohio State School for the Blind. They performed a braille version of Script Ohio as the Ohio State Marching Band conducted its customary routine. On September 3, 2011, a quadruple Script Ohio featured a record 768 marchers.

Script Ohio was named one of Athlon Sports' 10 Greatest College Football Traditions, along with the annual Army–Navy game, the Tournament of Roses, Notre Dame's Victory March, and Michigan's helmet, to name a few. It was voted among the top five traditions in an ESPN poll of college football coaches in October 2014. On ESPN's show, *Who's No. 1?* in 2006, Script Ohio was ranked as the top college football tradition.

Attend a Rose Bowl Game

Terrelle Pryor walked off of the field, rose tightly clenched by his jaw, reminiscent of how Ohio State had scraped by Iowa by the skin of its teeth, sending the Buckeyes to their first Rose Bowl in 13 years. Woody Hayes would have shrieked had he known his school would endure such a drought. Even when the Big Ten enforced a rule that prohibited a team from appearing in consecutive Rose Bowls, the Buckeyes expected to venture west to Pasadena, California, every other season. Once the conference lifted the mandate prior to the 1972 season, Ohio State expected to participate in the event on an annual basis.

So when 26-year-old walk-on kicker Devin Barclay sent the football spiraling through the uprights and vaulted the Buckeyes to a 27–24 overtime victory against the Iowa Hawkeyes on November 14, 2009, and the Ohio Stadium crowd of 105,455 poured out onto the field, it meant something. It meant a lot. Defensive lineman Doug Worthington called the victory "a storybook ending," and said the team was "on top of the world."

"None of our kids have gone to the Rose Bowl," said Ohio State head coach Jim Tressel.

John Hicks, an offensive lineman for Ohio State from 1970 to 1973, could not even make it 30 seconds into his Rose Bowl Hall of Fame speech in 2009 without breaking down in tears. Hicks' parents loved traveling to Pasadena for the game, which they did three times. Hicks became the first player to ever start in three Rose Bowls. His mother would begin saving up—mostly by winning at card games—for airplane tickets in October.

Coach Jim Tressel, left, and quarterback Terrelle Pryor, center, celebrate after victory in the 2010 Rose Bowl.

"It only cost $400, but she was hustling," Hicks said, laughing.

She would badger her son, asking if he was certain that Ohio State would earn the right to play in the New Year's Day affair. "You sure you're going to make it?" she would ask.

"And then here comes November," Hicks said. "'You guys going to make it?' She's over talking to Woody now. 'If they make it, how much is it going to cost?'"

During Hicks' three seasons with the Buckeyes, the team posted a 28–3–1 record and advanced to the Rose Bowl each season.

"To play in the Rose Bowl and be on national TV is the greatest thing my family ever, ever experienced," Hicks said before being overcome with emotion. "My mother and my father loved this place. It was

GRANDDADDY OF THEM ALL

Ohio State has participated in the Rose Bowl on 14 occasions. Here are the results from those games.

January 1, 1921: California 28, Ohio State 0
California did not lose a game from 1920 to 1924.

January 2, 1950: No. 6 Ohio State 17, No. 3 California 14
Because New Year's Day took place on a Sunday, the game was played on the Monday.

January 1, 1955: No. 1 Ohio State 20, No. 17 USC 7
The victory gave the 10–0 Buckeyes a split national championship with UCLA.

January 1, 1958: No. 2 Ohio State 10, Oregon 7
Oregon quarterback Jack Crabtree was named the game's Most Valuable Player, despite being on the losing end.

January 1, 1969: No. 1 Ohio State 27, No. 2 USC 16
In the second-ever Rose Bowl that pitted the nation's top two teams against each other, Ohio State overcame O.J. Simpson's 171 rushing yards by forcing five turnovers to complete an undefeated season.

January 1, 1971: No. 12 Stanford 27, No. 2 Ohio State 17
A win would have earned the unbeaten Buckeyes an undisputed national championship, but Stanford handed Ohio State its only loss of the season.

January 1, 1973: No. 1 USC 42, No. 3 Ohio State 17
The first of four consecutive Rose Bowl appearances for Ohio State proved to be a one-sided affair, as the Trojans sealed their undefeated season.

January 1, 1974: No. 4 Ohio State 42, No. 7 USC 21
The Buckeyes got revenge, as they scored the contest's final four touchdowns and finished the season with a 10–0–1 record.

January 1, 1975: No. 5 USC 18, No. 3 Ohio State 17
The Trojans converted a touchdown and two-point conversion in the fourth quarter to overtake Ohio State.

January 1, 1976: No. 11 UCLA 23, No. 1 Ohio State 10
The Buckeyes had walloped UCLA 41–20 three months earlier in Los Angeles, but the Bruins wrecked Ohio State's bid for a perfect season.

January 1, 1980: No. 3 USC 17, No. 1 Ohio State 16
USC running back Charles White rushed for 247 yards, including the game-winning one-yard touchdown with a little more than a minute remaining to mar the Buckeyes' unblemished record.

January 1, 1985: No. 18 USC 20, No. 6 Ohio State 17
Ohio State quarterback Mike Tomczak brought the Buckeyes to within three with a fourth-quarter touchdown pass and two-point conversion, but his three interceptions ultimately derailed the team's chances.

January 1, 1997: No. 4 Ohio State 20, No. 2 Arizona State 17
Buckeyes signal-caller Joe Germaine methodically moved Ohio State down the field in the last minute and his touchdown pass to David Boston spoiled the Sun Devils' perfect record.

January 1, 2010: No. 8 Ohio State 26, No. 7 Oregon 17
Ohio State quarterback Terrelle Pryor threw for a season-high 266 yards and tacked on 72 more on the ground to earn MVP honors.

the biggest trip they ever took in their life. This was the greatest, greatest place [my father] ever experienced in his life. And I felt very fortunate because I came three times and I played for one of the greatest people I've ever met in my life, Woody Hayes. It's hard not to be emotional about this, because it meant so much to all of us. They loved this place. It was a dream."

The winners of the Big Ten and Pac-12 used to earn the chance to play each other in the game each year. That conference affiliation is not as strong with the advent of the College Football Playoff, but the history and tradition remain intact. No scene is more picturesque than when the sun begins to set behind the mountains in the backdrop of the stadium, usually toward the end of the third quarter.

Ohio State has participated in 14 Rose Bowls and has amassed a 7–7 record. Michigan owns an 8–12 mark in 20 appearances. USC has played in the game a record 33 times and has racked up 24 wins and nine losses. The Wolverines smashed Stanford 49–0 in the first edition of the game in 1902, though at the time, it was referred to as the "Tournament East-West football game." It was not played again until 1916, but it has been played every year since. The 2014 edition marked the 100th Rose Bowl.

Six Ohio State players have been named Rose Bowl Most Valuable Player. Fullback Fred "Curly" Morrison merited the distinction in 1950. Quarterback Dave Leggett received the honor in 1955. Quarterback Rex Kern was named the game's MVP in 1969 to cap off the Buckeyes' unbeaten season. Quarterback Cornelius Greene earned the honor in 1974, as Ohio State finished a tie against Michigan away from a perfect year. Quarterback Joe Germaine captured the award after he engineered a last-minute touchdown drive to give the Buckeyes a comeback victory against Arizona State. Pryor garnered the accolade in 2010 following Ohio State's win against Oregon.

Each year since 1989, a group of players, coaches, athletic department executives, or other personnel involved in the game has been elected to the Rose Bowl Hall of Fame. Woody was included in the first induction class two years after his death. Running back Archie Griffin was enshrined in 1990. Kern joined the fold in 1991. Morrison was elected in 1993 and fullback Pete Johnson was inducted in 2007. Hicks was honored in 2009. Former head coach John Cooper was elected in 2012 and his old offensive tackle, Orlando Pace, followed suit in 2013. Hayes and Griffin were named as part of the All-Century Class in 2013. For that, Griffin participated in the 2014 Rose Parade, an annual march down Colorado Boulevard. Somewhere in the neighborhood of 40 floats and 20 marching bands complete the 5.5-mile trek the morning of the game. In all, the parade lasts a little more than two hours.

Rewatch "The Drive"

Jake Plummer slithered through the Ohio State defense and suddenly his nickname meant more than just a rhyming mechanism.

"Jake the Snake and the amazing Sun Devils of Arizona State have stated their case!" broadcaster Brent Musberger shouted.

With less than two minutes remaining in the 1997 Rose Bowl, Plummer dropped back and was swiftly swarmed by a group of battling linemen near the 20-yard line. He scooted away from the mob, escaped the grasp of a pair of Ohio State defenders, squirted free, and dove into the end zone. As he attempted to rise to his feet, a teammate jumped on his back and flattened him, his face planting in the gray-painted grass of Ohio State's end zone.

"The Snake does it again!" Musberger yelled. "This team won't die! You can cut a snake's head off, but he continues to live."

On third-and-goal from the 11-yard line, Plummer delivered the go-ahead score, offering another reminder of his innate ability to persevere in clutch moments.

"He's not like a rattlesnake," said Dick Vermeil, Musberger's partner on the broadcast. "He's more like a cobra."

"And when he strikes, it hurts," Musberger replied.

Luke Fickell, a defensive lineman for the Buckeyes, stood in the end zone with his hands on his hips and his head down, in a state of disbelief. Arizona State grabbed a 17–14 lead and stood a minute and a half from an undefeated season and likely at least a share of the national championship.

"If I were John Cooper right now, I would be almost ready to die," Vermeil said.

Quarterback Joe Germaine and the Buckeyes had 93 seconds to drive down the field and either tie the game with a field goal or win it with an improbable touchdown. The series began at the 35-yard line. On third-and-10, Germaine connected with receiver Dimitrious Stanley a few yards shy of midfield. As the clock ticked toward one minute, the effusive praise of Plummer from the broadcast booth continued.

"The Snake has done it again," Musberger said. "He did not win the Heisman, but you can certainly make a case that that man right there was the most valuable player in college football to his team this year. What I'm saying is entirely different. I'm certainly not arguing with the numbers Danny Wuerffel put up. What no one should forget is that this Arizona State team authored, in our mind, the biggest victory of the year early on, when they shut out Nebraska."

On another third-and-10, Germaine again hooked up with Stanley, whose catch moved the line of scrimmage to the Arizona State 41. On the ensuing snap, Germaine gained 11 yards with a quick toss to Stanley near the sideline. A pass interference call—following an Ohio State false start—shifted the football forward to the 20-yard line with 41 seconds remaining.

On first down, Germaine pump faked to his left before scrambling to his right. He passed up the opportunity to dash 10 or 15 yards ahead and instead lofted a pass beyond the reach of fullback Matt Keller. On second down, Germaine fired a pass toward Stanley at the 10-yard line, but defensive back Courtney Jackson intervened. Stanley pleaded for a pass interference call, but to no avail.

"Pass interference! Pass interference!" Vermeil yelled. "Jesus! Yeah, I would say that too, Stanley. It looked like he had a hold of him."

Jackson had hung on to Stanley's uniform as leverage as he swatted away the pass.

"The officials ought to donate their checks to charity on that call," Vermeil said. "My gosh. That's too obvious."

A play later, the officials rectified their mistake. On third-and-10, Arizona State was flagged for pass interference near the goal line as Sun Devils cornerback Marcus Soward wrapped his arms around the shoulders of freshman receiver David Boston before the football arrived. The infraction handed Ohio State a first-and-goal from the 5-yard line. Germaine dropped back to the 11, set himself, and heaved a pass to Boston, who had slipped out toward the right sideline and was standing all alone near the 1. He hauled in the throw, rotated his body, and waltzed into the end zone. With 19 seconds left, the Buckeyes had the lead.

Cooper raised both of his arms to signal the touchdown.

"You really can feel joy for this man," Musberger said, noting Cooper's 1–6 record in bowl games prior to the Rose Bowl.

Ohio State players embraced on the sideline. Arizona State players stood motionless and wide-eyed.

"It's a tough feeling to see them go ahead like that late in the game," Germaine said, "but we have confidence in ourselves that we can come back and make the plays and win the game."

The Sun Devils blocked Ohio State's extra-point try, but their desperation march down the field stalled out before they could attempt a field goal, as the clock struck zero and the Buckeyes captured their first Rose Bowl victory in 23 years. Ohio State finished the season with the No. 2 ranking in the nation.

"I've been coaching for 35 years," Cooper said, holding the Rose Bowl trophy. "Greatest victory in the history."

Learn the Ohio State Fight Songs

With the advent of Ohio Stadium two decades into the 20th century came a request for new school fight songs. The result was the Buckeye Battle Cry, a tune played after every Buckeyes score. The Ohio State Marching Band also performs part of the song at the end of its presentation of Script Ohio.

In old Ohio
There's a team
That's known throughout the land
Eleven warriors brave and bold
Whose fame will ever stand
And when the ball goes over

Our cheers will reach the sky
Ohio field will hear again
The Buckeye battle cry

Drive, drive on down that field
Men of the Scarlet and Gray
Don't let them through that line
We've got to win this game today
(O-hi-o)
Smash through to victory
We cheer you as you go
Our honor defend
So we'll fight to the end
For O-hi-o

The university adopted the song "Across the Field" for use in moments of rallying fans.

Fight the team across the field
Show them Ohio's here
Set the earth reverberating
With a mighty cheer
Hit them hard and see how they fall
Never let that team get the ball
Hail! Hail! The gang's all here
So let's win that old conference now

Scarlet vs. Green

It does not have the history nor the epic battles nor the vitriol that define Ohio State's rivalry with Michigan. The Buckeyes do have a burgeoning contention with Michigan State, however.

In fact, there have been enough tribulations between the two Big Ten titans to irk members from both sides. So much so that one Ohio State player has an uncommon wish born out of displeasure with a particular showing against the school from East Lansing, Michigan.

Fifteen years after a loss to Michigan State spoiled Ohio State's potential undefeated season, receiver Dee Miller quipped: "I wish they would change the color of money."

The former Buckeyes wideout loathes green more than he does maize and blue. On December 4, 2013, a friend showed Miller an old photo from Ohio State's November 1998 affair against Michigan State. December 4 happens to be Miller's birthday.

"I'm like, 'Dude, you just messed up my birthday,'" Miller said.

It is not water under a bridge. The grudge remains intact. The frustration continues to flow through the veins of anyone on Ohio State's side that afternoon at Ohio Stadium.

Miller, who said he never wears green, was the intended target on the Buckeyes' last gasp, a throw to the end zone on their final play. Michigan State cornerback Renaldo Hill stepped in front of Miller and intercepted Joe Germaine's desperate heave. Years after the fact, Miller's wide receivers coach with the Green Bay Packers, Charlie Baggett—who served as an assistant under head coach Nick Saban at Michigan State—told Miller the Spartans knew the exact route he was going to run on that last play.

"Maybe if it wasn't me they threw the ball to on the last play, I'd be like, 'Oh, well. We lost,'" Miller said. "But, no. I'm somewhat responsible for not making the play that we needed to make to stay undefeated and ranked No. 1."

The Buckeyes entered the contest as a 28-point favorite, having dismantled their previous eight opponents by an average of 29 points per game. But Michigan State roared back from a 24–9 deficit, scored the game's final 19 points, and forced five turnovers along the way. There was a somber postgame scene in Ohio State's locker room, typically the host to a confident, upbeat group. Miller said "it was like somebody died."

"It was ugly," said running back Jonathan Wells. "When you know that you're better than somebody but, unfortunately, on that day, they're better than you, you have to just live with it. It's a tough pill to swallow. It was tough. We were very disappointed. We were heartbroken. We had shown no signs of being beatable that season."

Neither Wells nor Miller has ever rewatched that game. Wells even admitted that he went 15 years without agreeing to an interview about the game.

"Even the next day, watching it on film just made me sick to my stomach," Miller said.

Fifteen years later, everything came full circle. In 1998, Michigan State dashed Ohio State's national title hopes in the inaugural season of the BCS system. In 2013, the final year of the BCS, the schools met again with a national championship game spot for the Buckeyes on the line. This time, the teams clashed at Lucas Oil Stadium in Indianapolis for the Big Ten Championship Game.

And again, the Spartans crushed the Buckeyes' championship dreams. They also snapped Ohio State's 24-game winning streak and handed head coach Urban Meyer his first loss as the head honcho in Columbus.

PLENTY OF TIES

If Ohio State and Michigan have acted as twin brothers routinely coming to blows and debating who is superior, then consider Michigan State the awkward third child longing for inclusion into the sibling rivalry. That child has barged its way into the discussion, though, especially given the recent disparity in stature between the chief competitors.

The Spartans, long looked upon as the Wolverines' kid brother and as one of "the other guys" in the Big Ten, have salvaged their image with a string of successful seasons under head coach Mark Dantonio. And Dantonio, of course, hails from Ohio and coached at Ohio State. He was raised in Zanesville, served as a graduate assistant for the Buckeyes in 1983–84 under Earle Bruce and returned to the school as defensive coordinator from 2001 to 2003 under Jim Tressel, who he worked with at Youngstown State from 1986 to 1990. Tressel coached the quarterbacks and receivers at Ohio State from 1983 to 1985.

There are many ties between Ohio State and Michigan State, two schools that have squared off in plenty of big games and spoiled each other's dream seasons. The Spartans marred the Buckeyes' unbeaten record in the 2013 conference championship game. A year later, Ohio State returned the favor in a trip to East Lansing, Michigan, in early November, when they handed Michigan State its first Big Ten loss in two years. The series dates back much earlier, though.

In 1970, Ohio State's only loss came in the Rose Bowl against Stanford. A year later, the Buckeyes had rattled off four straight conference wins. Then, Michigan State squeaked out a 17–10 win in Columbus. Woody Hayes' bunch proceeded to lose its next two contests, as well. In 1972, the unbeaten Buckeyes fell short 19–12 at Spartan Stadium in mid-November in their third-to-last game of the regular season. It proved to be Ohio State's only loss until the Rose Bowl. In 1974, the 4–3–1 Spartans topped the 8–0 Buckeyes—a No. 1-ranked team that had destroyed those eight opponents by an average score of 45–9—by a 16–13 final. It again marked Ohio State's only loss until the Rose Bowl. The Spartans served up their most significant upset in 1998, when they stormed back from a 19-point hole to stun the top-ranked Buckeyes 28–24 at Ohio Stadium in early November. That was the Buckeyes' only defeat that season. Nick Saban, the Spartans' head coach at the time, coached defensive backs at Ohio State from 1980 to 1981.

Overall, Ohio State has amassed a 29–14 record against Michigan State, including a 20–4 mark from 1975 to 2008. For much of the series history, the Buckeyes have entered the encounter as the favorite. Only twice since 1966 have the Spartans been the higher-ranked team at the time of kickoff.

Indianapolis was merely supposed to be the layover. In the itinerary that Urban Meyer and Ohio State mapped out two years earlier, the final destination was marked as Pasadena, California, and not for a New Year's Day soiree.

No, the Buckeyes' ideal travel agenda, first sketched out at the tail end of 2011, culminated in a trip to the BCS Championship Game on the first Monday of 2014. Their plans did not match those of Michigan State, though.

The Spartans scored the contest's final 17 points and stuffed Braxton Miller on a quarterback rush to the right side on a critical fourth-quarter fourth-down play. The Buckeyes could not shake the ghosts of upsets past. They rushed for 273 yards against the nation's top-ranked defense. They erased their largest deficit of the season, a 17–0 hole in the first half. Despite designation as the "road team," they played before a scarlet-painted crowd.

And yet, it was Michigan State hoisting the Stagg Championship Trophy before exiting Lucas Oil Stadium following a 34–24 upset of Ohio State, one eerily reminiscent of the damage done in Columbus 15 years earlier.

Those national title hopes? Dashed. Ohio State's defense? Gashed. The seemingly inevitable Florida State–Ohio State party in Pasadena? Crashed. The Spartans rerouted Ohio State to south Florida for the Orange Bowl, a far less desirable consolation prize. Senior center Corey Linsley described it as "a reality check."

"They're obviously a good team, but it was like we were playing the Bears or something," Linsley said.

Meyer answered questions during his postgame press conference with his head down, buried in the microphone, and with his voice quivering. He said the loss would "haunt all of us, I imagine, for a little while." For the first time in his two years as Ohio State head coach, he seemed vulnerable and mortal. His team looked the same way on the field for the previous three-plus hours. Meyer said he took the loss harder than normal because he wanted his players "to experience something special." A trip to the Orange Bowl did not qualify, given his standards, established when he assumed the head coaching position at Ohio State two years prior.

"I could tell it was tough on him because we all expected to go to the national championship and win that game," said linebacker Ryan Shazier. "It was tough on all of us. We all handled it pretty much the same. We just stayed close to each other and we hung out with the people that are most important to us."

The days after were dark, lonely, solemn, and discomforting.

Shazier watched the game film over and over. He lay in his bed, contemplating the same two questions.

"How did this happen?"

"Why did this happen?"

The Buckeyes expected a battle with Michigan State. They didn't expect to fall short in their fight for a national championship game berth.

"I just couldn't stop thinking about it because it felt so unreal," Shazier said.

Just as Miller could not erase memories of his pattern to the end zone on the final play, Ohio State tight end Jeff Heuerman was haunted by a missed block that could have sprung Miller loose on the fourth-down attempt. Trailing 27–24 with about six minutes remaining, Ohio State possessed the ball in Michigan State territory. Meyer called a timeout before the play to devise a strategy. A fresh set of downs would have altered the landscape of the game. The Buckeyes needed two yards.

"Coulda, woulda, shoulda," Linsley said. "That was the game."

Heuerman repositioned himself to the right side of the offensive line. Miller took the snap and darted to his right, but Spartans linebacker Denicos Allen, an All-Big Ten selection, sprung out of Heuerman's grasp and dragged Miller to the ground, short of the chains. Heuerman, who credited Allen for making a "good play," said he thought about the sequence of events "about a million times" in the week following the defeat.

"I beat myself up a little bit," Heuerman said. "I think every competitive athlete does. I don't think you can shake a play like that or a game like that, especially the outcome. You have to keep moving. Grown men, they get up the next day and go about their business. You can't dread on the past."

Michigan State quarterback Connor Cook took a knee with 30 seconds left and the Spartans spilled out onto the field, a Rose Bowl berth in hand for the first time in a quarter-century.

"It sucks," Linsley said.

At last, the Buckeyes earned vindication in 2014. They walloped Michigan State 49–24 at Spartan Stadium on Nov. 8, a victory that vaulted them back into the national title conversation. It marked the first signature win for a team that proceeded to march to the first College Football Championship.

. . . .

Watch a Game from a Buckeye Backer Bar

Close to 500,000 Ohio State alumni are spread throughout the world and about half of them live outside of the state of Ohio. Buckeyes are everywhere, from Columbus to California to New York City to Texas to Europe and Asia and South America. For that reason, there are particular establishments in many cities across the map that serve as Ohio State rendezvous points. There are enough alumni in certain cities such as Chicago and Los Angeles that a distinct restaurant or bar might be filled to capacity with patrons wearing scarlet and gray on any given Saturday.

The Ohio State Alumni Association has recommendations on specific establishments in nearly every U.S. state, as well as in Brazil, China, Canada, England, Italy, and Japan. Even in Anchorage, Alaska, one can trek to The Peanut Farm. Here are a handful of Buckeye Backers bars to venture to if you're ever in these areas at the time of the opening kickoff or tipoff.

Chicago
McGee's Tavern & Grille

Where: 950 W. Webster Ave., Chicago, Illinois, 60614

Located in Lincoln Park, McGee's is renowned for its Irish pub fare, with fish and chips, corned beef, pizza, and sandwiches. On

Saturdays, the restaurant serves beer in "Big Buckeye mugs." There are fan giveaways, renditions of "Hang on Sloopy," and all of the traditional fanfare that any Ohio State alumnus seeks when watching a game with fellow Buckeyes.

Los Angeles
The Happy Ending Bar and Restaurant

Where: 7038 West Sunset Blvd., Los Angeles, California, 90028

In October 2007, The Happy Ending opened in Hollywood with the intent of appealing to those who value "fun and comfort over exclusivity and pretension." The goal was to create an upscale New York dive bar feel, but serve to those craving "global comfort food" and welcome sports fans, too. The restaurant's menu is highlighted by filet mignon sliders, buffalo chicken spring rolls, chicken parmesan, Sicilian style pizza, New York specialty sandwiches, and the Smore's platter dessert. The 10,000 square-foot location includes more than 50 plasma TVs and considers itself the official home for fans of the New York Giants, Ohio State Buckeyes, Miami Hurricanes, and Nebraska Cornhuskers.

Dallas/Fort Worth
Austin Avenue Grill & Sports Bar

Where: 1801 N. Plano Road, Richardson, Texas, 75081

The restaurant hosts fans of Ohio State football, Kentucky basketball, and the Pittsburgh Steelers. Its menu contains a wide variety of food, from traditional pub fare to a peanut butter burger to fajitas to pasta primavera.

Woody's Sports Restaurant

Where: 307 W. Main Street, Frisco, Texas, 75034

The name should give it away. If it does not, they have a message on their website: "We're Ohio State fans so Buckeyes are always welcome!" Woody's, which has a scarlet and gray color scheme, features 15 beers on tap, four 10-foot projection screens, and 11 high-definition flat-screen TVs. The menu includes a handful of salad options, an extensive appetizers list, burgers, sandwiches, wings, shrimp, chicken, salmon, ribs, and more.

Miami
Miller's North Miami Beach Ale House

Where: 3227 Northeast 163rd Street, North Miami Beach, Florida, 33160

The Ale House offers more than 75 brands of beer and has an extensive menu that includes everything from a New York strip steak to lobster to pastas to salads to ribs to jambalaya to flatbreads to fajitas. They promote their Zingers—essentially breaded chicken tenders basted in one of a number of sauce choices—as their calling card. The chain restaurant has been around since 1988. One location opened at the corner of 3rd Avenue and Olentangy River Road in 2013.

New York City
Iron Bar

Where: The corner of 45th Street and 8th Ave., New York, New York, 10036

Just a block from Times Square, the 5,000 square-foot space has 45 draft beers on tap and 45 more in bottled form. Twenty TVs prominently display the Ohio State football games on Saturday afternoons, as does a 16-foot-wide projector in a lounge area with plenty of sofas. The gastropub serves typical bar food, in addition to salads, burgers, and pizzas.

Chapter 5

Basketball and Other Sports

Hoops School

The football team garners all of the glory in Columbus, but Ohio State's men's basketball team has constructed quite a history over the years. College stars and eventual NBA talents have made pit stops on campus and have helped the Buckeyes establish themselves as perennial NCAA title contenders. Of course, the program only has one championship to boast. In 1960, Fred Taylor's team, led by Jerry Lucas and John Havlicek, toppled California by 20 points in the title game in the Golden Bears' backyard near San Francisco. The team reached the national final in each of the two following seasons, but the Buckeyes fell short against the University of Cincinnati.

Ohio State has reached the Final Four on four occasions since. In 1968, the Buckeyes lost to North Carolina, who lost in the title game to John Wooden's UCLA squad that was anchored by Lew Alcindor. As a No. 4 seed in 1999, Jim O'Brien's bunch advanced to the Final Four before suffering a six-point defeat against eventual champion Connecticut. Backcourt mates Scoonie Penn and Michael Redd carried the team to an upset of No. 1 Auburn in the Sweet 16 and No. 3 St. John's in the regional final.

In 2007, Thad Matta directed a young, talented team to the title game. Seven-foot freshman center Greg Oden provided a post presence that gave opponents fits. Freshman point guard Mike Conley carved up defenses with his pinpoint passing. Guards Jamar Butler, Daequan Cook, and Ron Lewis offered outside shooting. Forwards David Lighty, Ivan Harris, and Othello Hunter contributed some muscle. The group nearly suffered an early exit from the NCAA Tournament. A desperation 3-pointer from Lewis forced the Buckeyes' second-round matchup against Xavier to an extra period. Ohio State won by seven in overtime. In the regional semifinal, the Buckeyes overcame a 17-point halftime deficit against Tennessee and won by a single point. In the title game, Billy Donovan's Florida team proved too experienced and balanced, as four starters scored in double figures to lead the Gators to their second consecutive national championship.

As a No. 2 seed, the Buckeyes marched to the Final Four in 2012 before falling short in a close contest against Kansas. Matta's crew, led by sophomores Jared Sullinger, Deshaun Thomas, and Aaron Craft, and senior William Buford, knocked off top-seeded Syracuse in the regional final to advance to New Orleans. There, Ohio State held a nine-point advantage at intermission and Kansas led the game for fewer than four minutes, but the Jayhawks clamped down defensively, knocked down a handful of late free throws, and captured the victory.

In all, Ohio State has qualified for the NCAA Tournament on 31 occasions. The Buckeyes have made 11 Final Four appearances

Down the street from Ohio Stadium rests the Schottenstein Center, the home to Ohio State's basketball team.

SCORING RECORDS

Here is a sampling of the program's scoring records.

Most points scored in a career:
1. Dennis Hopson: 2,096 (1983–87, 125 games)
2. Herb Williams: 2,011 (1977–81, 114 games)
3. (tie) William Buford: 1,990 (2008–12, 145 games)
   Jerry Lucas: 1,990 (1959–62, 82 games)
5. Kelvin Ransey: 1,934 (1976–80, 112 games)
6. Michael Redd: 1,879 (1997–00, 96 games)
7. Jim Jackson: 1,785 (1989–92, 93 games)
8. Jay Burson: 1,756 (1985–89, 122 games)
9. Deshaun Thomas: 1,630 (2010–13, 113 games)
10. Dave Sorenson: 1,622 (1967–70, 77 games)

Most points per game for a season:
1. Robin Freeman: 32.9 (1956)
2. Gary Bradds: 30.6 (1964)
3. Dennis Hopson: 29.0 (1987)
4. Gary Bradds: 28.0 (1963)
5. Jerry Lucas: 26.3 (1960)
6. Jerry Lucas: 24.8 (1961)
7. Dave Sorenson: 24.2 (1970)
8. Alan Hornyak: 24.0 (1973)
9. Dave Sorenson: 23.6 (1969)
10. Paul Ebert: 23.4 (1954)

Most rebounds recorded in a career:

1. Jerry Lucas: 1,411 (1959–62)
2. Herb Williams: 1,111 (1977–81)
3. Perry Carter: 989 (1987–91)
4. Bill Hosket Jr.: 910 (1965–68)
5. Terence Dials: 876 (2001–06)
6. Clark Kellogg: 872 (1979–82)
7. Luke Witte: 819 (1970–73)
8. Dave Sorenson: 761 (1967–70)
9. Ken Johnson: 739 (1997–01)
10. John Havlicek: 720 (1959–62)

and have finished as the tournament's runner-up four times (1939, 1961, 1962 and 2007). Ohio State has claimed 22 regular-season conference championships and five Big Ten Tournament championships. Football reigns supreme in Columbus, but the frigid winters and chilly springs in central Ohio have often been met with quality college basketball.

. . . .

Learn about the Wonder Kids

When Jerry Lucas and John Havlicek arrived at Ohio State, everything changed. Suddenly, the freshman basketball team could beat the varsity squad. Lucas and Havlicek led the way, and when they placed their first year on campus in the rearview, Ohio State basketball hit the map. Lucas instantly became the focal point of the Buckeyes offensive attack. During the 1959–60 season—his first on the varsity team—Lucas averaged 26.3 points and 16.4 rebounds per game, while shooting nearly 64 percent from the floor. Havlicek chipped in 12.2 points and 7.3 rebounds per contest. Ohio State won the national championship that season. A year later, they cruised to the title game again—carrying with them a 27–0 record—but they lost 70–65 to Cincinnati, a result that still haunts Lucas. The Buckeyes made it back to the national championship game in 1962 and again, Cincinnati emerged victorious.

Lucas averaged 24.9 points and 17.4 rebounds per game as a junior and 21.8 points and 17.8 rebounds per contest as a senior. He was named a consensus All-American in all three of his seasons. He was twice named the Most Outstanding Player of the Final Four and twice named the Associated Press Player of the Year.

Before Havlicek ever stole the ball for the Celtics, he averaged 14.5 points and 8.7 rebounds per game as a junior and 17 points and 9.7 rebounds per game as a senior. His efforts during his final year in scarlet and gray earned him a place on the All-America second team.

Both players prospered in the NBA. Lucas made seven All-Star teams, averaged 17 points and 15.6 rebounds per affair, and won a championship with the New York Knicks in 1973. Havlicek was selected to 13 All-Star games and won eight championship rings with the Boston Celtics.

"During a lull in a game that we were doing," said longtime college basketball coach Bob Knight, "[commentator] Brent Musberger said to me, 'If you had to pick one guy to take the most important shot, who would it be?' I said it would be Havlicek. I saw him do that his entire career."

The King's Court

omeone who identifies as a diehard Ohio State fan ought to know the school's colors. So when LeBron James once referred to his favorite school as the "scarlet and red," it made every Buckeyes backer on the planet cringe a bit.

The basketball star has had a rocky relationship with the university's loyal supporters. Many Ohio State alumni hail from the northeast sector of the state, the area he vacated for four years during his tenure with the Miami Heat. James' devotion to Ohio State, however, has never wavered.

He has long maintained that had he attended college, he would have chosen Ohio State. He cites Eddie George and Joey Galloway and Akron, Ohio, native Antoine Winfield as the football players for whom he rooted while growing up. Over time, he developed relationships with football coach Urban Meyer, basketball coach Thad Matta, and athletic director Gene Smith. He built friendships with quarterbacks Terrelle Pryor and Braxton Miller. He has watched parts of football games from Smith's suite on the press level of Ohio Stadium. Meyer reached out to James to welcome him back to the Buckeye State when the superstar announced his intention to return to the Cleveland Cavaliers in July 2014.

James has his own locker inside the Buckeyes' locker room at the Schottenstein Center. It was constructed in 2013 as part of the $19 million expansion of the basketball team's practice facilities. His nameplate displays his old No. 6, his hometown of Akron, and his moniker next to an Ohio State logo. The locker room itself is named after former Buckeye and NBA shooting guard Michael Redd, who donated $500,000 toward the renovations.

The team presented James with a jersey prior to a Cavaliers preseason game that took place at the Columbus arena. The Cavs typically play one preseason game each year at the Schottenstein Center. James even worked out at the team's facilities during the 2011 NBA lockout. In 2007, the basketball team began to sport James' Nike gear rather than the company's patented swoosh symbol.

He has spoken to both the football and basketball teams as a means of an occasional motivational message. Before a nationally televised night game against Wisconsin in September 2013, James spoke at the Skull Session pep rally.

"I promise, I say this all the time—if I had one year of college, I would have ended up here," he said. James led the team down the steps outside the Blackwell Hotel to St. John Arena, where Meyer introduced him to mostly cheers, but a few noticeable boos.

"[He's] one of, arguably, the greatest champions, greatest competitors and most importantly, a Buckeye," Meyer said. "To have him come and be gracious with our team, visit our team, speak to our team—he loves Ohio State."

James typically attends an Ohio State football game each year and he often cheers loudly for them on social media. While wrapping up his recovery from a balky lower back and knee, he used his off day between games at Sacramento and at Phoenix to attend the Buckeyes' bout with Oregon in the inaugural College Football Playoff Championship Game at AT&T Stadium in Arlington, Texas, in January 2015. He wore a white alternate No. 23 jersey, the uniforms the team donned for its meeting with Michigan in 2009.

Following Ohio State's 42–20 triumph against the Ducks, James recorded a two-minute video message for the team from the friendly confines of his personal jet as he traveled back to Phoenix. In it, he commended Meyer; quarterbacks Cardale Jones, Braxton Miller, and J.T. Barrett; running back Ezekiel Elliott, receiver Devin Smith,. and others.

"I want to say congratulations to the Ohio State Buckeyes," James said, his voice hoarse from screaming during the game. "Coach Meyer, you are unbelievable. We're happy to have you. I can't say too many words. You guys are unbelievable. Congratulations on this whole journey. Braxton Miller and J.T. Barrett, you guys got it started. The coaching staff, everyone played a part in you guys winning this national championship.

"I don't know if people know how much this means for the state of Ohio. This is for everyone in Ohio, because we're always counted out. Always. For you guys to lose that first game to Virginia Tech, to come all the way back, to be counted out against Wisconsin in the Big Ten Championship, to be counted out versus Alabama in the [semifinals] and to be counted out once again in the finals versus Oregon, just shows that the critics and the naysayers and the so-called experts don't mean anything.

"Once you get inside those lines, that's when the real game starts. You guys showed what it means to be a true champion. As a guy being from Ohio who has supported you guys, I love you. It's unbelievable. So many emotions. I couldn't be more proud of all of you guys, every last one of you guys."

A few days earlier, James provided every player on the team with a pair of Beats by Dre headphones. Technically, he just helped facilitate "a donation" so as not to violate NCAA rules. Of course, the headphones were not scarlet or gray. They were red. One day, he will get the color scheme down.

"No matter where I go in the world, no matter where it is," James said prior to that Wisconsin game in 2013, "I will always rock Ohio State colors."

Or at least something close to it.

The Man Who Did Everything: Evan Turner

Evan Turner was buying some bread at Wal-Mart. That is where he was recognized by some fellow shoppers who asked about his back injury and when he might return to the basketball court. Turner contended that he would be back in Thad Matta's starting lineup in three weeks, which would put his return at about five weeks after he fractured a pair of vertebrae in his spine when he hit the floor with a thud following a dunk attempt on December 5, 2009. Sure enough, Turner was back on the court right when he promised, three weeks earlier than doctors had initially projected.

Against Eastern Michigan, Turner lost his grip on the rim after slicing down the lane for a throwdown. The ball ricocheted off the rim, too, and Turner fell straight on his back, his legs up in the air. He immediately rolled over onto his chest, slammed the baseline with his right hand, let out a scream, and writhed around in pain.

At first glance, it looked like the type of injury that could derail a player's season or career. Instead, it cost Turner about a month. Fortunately for the junior swingman and for the Buckeyes, he still had plenty of time to put the finishing touches on a record-setting season in Columbus.

Legendary coach Bob Knight told Turner: "You have to promise me you won't try and dunk the ball anymore. When you dunk it, just lay it up there and push it down through."

"He tried a little bit of a Broadway dunk and that could have really crippled this team, because he's a hell of a player," Knight said.

Evan Turner was named the National Player of the Year after the 2009–10 season.

Turner averaged 17.3 points per game as a sophomore for an Ohio State team that was bounced by Siena in the first round of the NCAA Tournament. A year later, Turner took over more of the ball-handling duties and he averaged 20.4 points, 9.2 rebounds, six assists, and nearly two steals per contest. He shot 54 percent from the field and he recorded two triple doubles. He was a consensus first-team All-American and was selected as the National Player of the Year.

His Ohio State career ended in a less than ideal fashion, however. Turner sat at center court at the Edward Jones Dome in St. Louis, mesmerized. Several of his teammates ventured over to him, offering to help him to his feet, but he refused their assistance. He opted to bypass postgame handshakes and instead headed directly for the locker room. The reality of a hard-fought, season-ending loss did not take long to sink in as he competed in scarlet and gray for the final time in the No. 2 Buckeyes' 76–73 loss to No. 6 Tennessee in a battle for a spot in the Elite Eight in 2010.

The meeting marked the fourth between the two schools in a three-year span. All four affairs were decided by five points or fewer. In this instance, the Volunteers clenched a three-point lead as Ohio State possessed the ball with 12 seconds remaining. Turner had two looks at the basket, but both shots—and the Buckeyes as a whole—fell short.

"You want the ball in the hands of your best player," said sharpshooter Jon Diebler, who referred to Turner as the "best player in the country." "We will live with having the ball in the best player's hands with 12 seconds left."

Turner thought he was fouled, but the referees left their whistles on silent. The loss served as the final chapter in a storied collegiate career. Appropriately, he stuffed the stat sheet in his last hurrah, with 31 points, seven rebounds, and five assists. A few weeks later, with his voice quivering while speaking inside the auxiliary gym at the Schottenstein Center, Turner announced his intention to forgo his senior season and declare for the NBA Draft. He said he agonized over the decision and referred to it as "the toughest thing" he ever had to do. He said he wished he could "really just disappear." Eventually, though, the Philadelphia 76ers selected him with the No. 2 pick in the draft. He called his career at Ohio State and the opportunity to advance to the next level "a dream come true."

"I had the most fun I've ever had playing basketball," he said. "I think we grew as a team. We genuinely care for each other and have a lot of fun. To overcome the situations we had, [we] proved a lot of people wrong and just believing in each other was one of the best times of my life."

The Scoring Machine: Dennis Hopson

In a 1986 contest against Ohio University, Dennis Hopson tallied 27 points, 11 rebounds, and 10 assists, as he registered the first triple double in Ohio State history. That feat stood for nearly a quarter-century before Evan Turner logged one of his own. Hopson has long been the scoring standard at Ohio State, though. He scored the most points in program history, eclipsing Herb Williams' total near the end of his senior year. He also averaged 8.2 rebounds per game that season, an impressive statistic for a 6'5" swingman. Those numbers—he finished second in scoring among Division I players—helped him garner the Big Ten Player of the Year award in 1987, and he was also named to the All-America second team.

Waste Away in "Mattaritaville"

This is not what Jimmy Buffett had in mind.

Ohio State is widely recognized as a football school, but no one camps out in the parking lot surrounding The Horseshoe, braving the arctic temperatures in anticipation of the opening of the venue's gates. In 2013, Ohio State students created Mattaritaville, an homage to both Buffett and men's basketball coach Thad Matta and a tradition of building up the hype for the most critical of the team's contests. It is a common practice at renowned basketball schools such as Duke, where students camp out for weeks at a time.

Student season-ticket packages at Ohio State come with general admission seating, so the sooner one arrives at the arena, the better seat one can claim. Therefore, a few days before each big basketball game, students line up tents along the outside walls of the Schottenstein Center and camp out in anticipation. Typically, 20 or more tents can be found parked on the sidewalk. The students dubbed the area Mattaritaville, a play off of Matta's last name and Buffett's classic song, "Margaritaville."

Occasionally, players or coaches from the basketball or football team will reward the diligent fans with food or drinks for their troubles. With basketball season taking place in the winter, students are often tasked with bearing the freezing temperatures and occasional snowfall. The organization's Facebook page includes a profile picture of Matta, with his thumbs up, donning a Hawaiian shirt and a lei. Typically, the students wear nothing of that sort. They can often

The Schottenstein Center houses the Buckeye Nuthouse, the student section at men's basketball games.

be seen, thanks to Mother Nature, sporting scarves, parkas, boots, and gloves. At least one person must occupy each tent at all times. Security guards at the arena will occasionally allow students to use the bathrooms in the facility. Students plug in their electronics to outlets on the side of the building. Two hours before tip-off, the students can finally enter the inside of the arena, at that point a sanctuary of warmth and salvation.

· ·

The Lefty: Michael Redd

The Ohio State basketball locker room bears Michael Redd's name for a reason. Well, really, for 500,000 reasons, as the former sharpshooter's donation to the renovations of the team's facilities fueled the dedication. If there were a 500,001st reason, it would be what Redd accomplished while wearing scarlet and gray. The 6-foot-6 southpaw had a sweet shooting stroke that allowed him to average 21.9 points per game as a freshman, 19.5 as a sophomore, and 17.3 as a junior. He led the Big Ten in scoring in each of his first two years at Ohio State and he was named the Big Ten Freshman of the Year in 1998. He blossomed in the NBA with the Milwaukee Bucks, as he became a prolific scorer before knee injuries took their toll on him.

· ·

The Boy Who Never Did Wrong: Aaron Craft

Aaron Craft's offseason resembled that of any typical 22-year-old. He took classes. He journeyed through Haiti on a mission trip. He got engaged to his longtime girlfriend. And, of course, his roommates chronicled all of the happenings on Twitter. You know, all of the usual stuff.

The moment Ohio State's point guard returned to Columbus and readied for a new slate of practices and coursework, it dawned on him. This is it.

"It starts hitting you," Craft said. "You start realizing it's coming to an end."

The undersized, overmatched guard—on paper, at least—who had seemingly been at the school forever was finally entering his last season in scarlet and gray. He had built a reputation as the rosy-cheeked boy who never did wrong. He played near-perfect defense, suffocating opposing ball handlers who feared to dribble within his reach. He operated Thad Matta's offense, finding teammates in the proper spots to set themselves for a high-percentage shot. He stayed out of trouble off of the court and said all of the right things to the media. He preached about the value of his Christian faith. He planned to go to medical school if a chance at the NBA never materialized.

The summer before his senior season, he spent a week traversing the streets of Haiti, where he spoke with villagers via a translator and gained an overwhelming sense of perspective.

"It was a great experience, but at the same time, it was still pretty heartbreaking," Craft said. "I saw what people have to deal with down there on a daily basis. It's hot. There's no electricity. It's tough to come by water. That's just stuff we take for granted every day."

Craft referred to the voyage as the "perfect way to springboard" into his senior year of college and his final season of basketball, one he planned to cherish and treasure.

"It really opened my eyes to see how blessed we are to be here," Craft said. "For me to be able to play at Ohio State and get the things that I do and experience the things I get to experience, it just took it to a whole different level."

The journey provided Craft with newfound motivation for his senior year. He spent much of the offseason refining his jump shot in an effort to improve on the 42 percent mark from the floor he posted as a junior. He converted 47 percent of his shots as a senior. Despite that statistic as a junior, he still earned his way onto the All-Big Ten second team and was the conference tournament's Most Outstanding Player. He knocked down the game-winning 3-pointer in Ohio State's triumph over Iowa State in the NCAA Tournament, a victory that advanced the Buckeyes to the Sweet 16.

"[He's] the one person that you don't have to challenge to get the job done," Matta said. "Since his freshman year, I never thought one time about [needing to] motivate him."

Craft always motivated others, though. Matta said he noticed a more vocal approach to leadership from his point guard during his senior season. That year, Craft was selected to the All-Big Ten third team. He was named the Big Ten's Defensive Player of the Year for the second time and earned his way onto the conference's All-Defensive Team for the fourth straight year. He became the fourth player in league history to be named to the Academic All-America first team on three occasions and the third athlete in history to twice claim the distinction of Academic All-American of the Year.

· ·

The Backside: Jared Sullinger

Jared Sullinger always said his greatest asset was his posterior. His bulky backside allowed him to obtain positioning on his defender near the basket and he excelled around the rim during his two years at Ohio State. The power forward averaged 17.2 points and 10.2 rebounds per game as a freshman in 2010–11. The next year, he recorded marks of 17.5 points and 9.2 rebounds per contest. The Buckeyes reached the Sweet 16 as a No. 1 seed, but lost to No. 4 seed Kentucky 62–60 when William Buford's 3-point attempt clanked off the rim in the waning seconds. A year later, Ohio State advanced to the Final Four, but the Buckeyes surrendered a nine-point halftime lead and fell short against Kansas by a 64–62 final. Sullinger, who had racked up 21 points and 16 rebounds against Kentucky a year earlier, shot 5 of 19 against the Jayhawks and was limited to 13 points and 11 boards.

Eat Some Chicken Fingers from Raising Cane's

WHERE: 1816 N. High Street, Columbus, Ohio, 43201

WHEN: 10:30 AM to 11:00 PM Sunday through Wednesday; 10:30 AM to 3:00 AM Thursday through Saturday

HOW TO DO IT: Stop in, order at the counter, and grab your hot food a couple of minutes later

COST FACTOR: A traditional Box Combo, with four chicken fingers, fries, coleslaw, Cane's Sauce, Texas toast, and a drink costs between $6-7; chicken fingers can be ordered individually for about $1 apiece

BUCKET RANK:

· ·

The menu is simple and concise. The food is far from fancy. And yet, stroll past Raising Cane's late on a Friday or Saturday night and the line will extend through the heart of the restaurant and spill out onto High Street.

Some come for the fresh, juicy chicken fingers, the staple of the company, first established in 1996 on the campus of LSU. Some enjoy the crinkle-cut french fries. Many just want the slab of Texas toast that accompanies every meal order. Few can go without the heralded Cane's Sauce, a tangy condiment that can top any of the three aforementioned items. The restaurant employs a top-secret recipe for its sauce.

Situated on the always-bustling High Street directly across from the center of Ohio State's campus provides Raising Cane's with a steady flow of foot traffic. Business, however, tends to reach a crescendo during the weekend's after-hours. Whether it is a matter of students needing substance to accommodate their liquor-filled bellies or needing a late-night snack to keep them awake, the place is often packed past capacity and staffed with extra security. This particular location is dubbed "The Late Show" and stays open until 3:00 AM on Thursday through Saturday. Chicken finger cravers might arrive at the spot well after midnight and still be forced to wait in line for an hour or so.

The High Street location, the franchise's first in the state of Ohio, opened on October 27, 2004. There are a handful of Columbus locations, including one on Olentangy River Road, down the street from the Schottenstein Center, where Ohio State's basketball teams play, and the Woody Hayes Athletic Center, where Ohio State's football team practices and studies film.

Raising Cane's paints its patrons as "Caniacs." These creatures seem to come out most often at night on the weekends at the campus location.

The chicken fingers at Raising Cane's are a popular item among Ohio State students.

The Swingman: Jim Jackson

It took Ohio State nearly a decade to retire Jim Jackson's No. 22. Jackson was not one to wait around. During his freshman season with the Buckeyes in 1989–90, Jackson averaged 16.1 points, 5.5 rebounds, and 3.7 assists per game. As a sophomore, he upped his averages to 18.9 points, 5.5 rebounds, and 4.3 assists per contest. That year, he helped guide Ohio State to a No. 1 seed in the NCAA Tournament. The Buckeyes reached the Sweet 16 before bowing out against fourth-seeded St. John's. Jackson averaged 22.4 points, 6.8 rebounds, and four assists per game as a junior, his final season in Columbus. Ohio State once again earned a top seed and reached the Elite Eight before falling short by four points against Michigan's Fab Five.

Visit the Jack Nicklaus Museum

WHERE: 2355 Olentangy River Road, Columbus, Ohio, 43210

WHEN: Tuesday through Saturday, 9:00 AM to 5:00 PM

HOW TO DO IT: Open to the public, with parking right in front of the building

COST FACTOR: Admission is $10 for adults, or $5 for students with a valid Ohio State ID card

BUCKET RANK: 🪣 🪣

Nestled between the Schottenstein Center and the Woody Hayes Athletic Center is the Jack Nicklaus Museum, home to plenty of artifacts celebrating the career of the golf icon.

Nestled between Ohio State's basketball arena and football complex is a brick building that hosts evidence of perhaps the most dominant professional athlete ever to graduate from the university. It is not a gallery full of hardware from the countless All-Americans who cycled through the football program under Woody Hayes, Earle Bruce, John Cooper, and Jim Tressel. It is not an institution that holds banners from Final Four trips.

The oft-overlooked sanctuary serves as a home to the litany of honors and achievements captured by perhaps the greatest golfer in the history of the sport. The Jack Nicklaus Museum, a 24,000 square-foot vault of The Golden Bear's triumphs, opened in 2002.

Walk into the foyer and Nicklaus' accomplishments immediately pop up. Plaques and awards scatter the walls of the entry room. To the left is a large theater, where Tressel used to hold his weekly session with the media. To the right is a gallery that takes visitors through Nicklaus' life by the decade. Learn about his youth in the 1940s, how he started to grasp the game in the 1950s, his rise to prominence in the 1960s, his run of dominance in the 1970s, and so on. Golf clubs and balls, trophies, scorecards, and awards adorn each display.

In an adjacent area, the story of Nicklaus' 18 PGA Tour major championship victories (and two amateur titles) is told through trophies and green jackets and golf clubs. Murals of each championship site are painted on the walls. Nicklaus claimed six Masters titles, four U.S. Open championships, three British Open crowns, and five PGA Championship titles. His 18 major championships remain the PGA Tour record.

In the back corner of the museum sits the Nicklaus Family Room, a den full of family mementos. Nicklaus and his wife, Barbara, have five children and 22 grandchildren. On a TV in the center of the back wall, Nicklaus' son, Jack, offers an inside look at growing up in the family household in Florida.

Nicklaus designed the course layout at Muirfield Village Golf Club in Columbus. The course opened in 1974 and has hosted the Memorial Tournament since 1976. The Jack Nicklaus Museum contains an exhibit dedicated to the tournament, with displays featuring event highlights, tournament information, past champions, and annual honorees. An adjacent room highlights Nicklaus' affinity for designing courses. He has designed nearly 300 across the world and they are all documented on a giant map.

The Legends of Golf Gallery scripts the history of the sport. Highlighted are the origins of the game in the 1400s in Scotland and some of golf's pioneers and superstars, including Sam Snead, Ben

Hogan, and Arnold Palmer. The gallery also details the sport's ever-evolving equipment.

Another corridor flaunts paintings of Nicklaus by artist Glenn Harrington. The portraits serve as an essay of Nicklaus' career and family life through the years. The museum also hosts a history of Ohio State's golf programs, a pro shop, and a traveling exhibit gallery.

Nicklaus posted 73 official PGA Tour victories. He was enshrined into the World Golf Hall of Fame in 1974. He was named golfer of the decade and athlete of the decade by numerous outlets in the 1970s. *Golf* magazine and the Associated Press were among a slew of outlets that dubbed him the Golfer of the Century. *Sports Illustrated* took it one step further, classifying him as the best individual male athlete of the 20th century. *Golf Digest* tagged him as the greatest golfer of all time.

On March 24, 2015, Nicklaus was awarded the congressional gold medal in Washington, D.C. He became the seventh athlete in history to receive the honor and the second Ohio State athlete. Track star Jesse Owens was posthumously honored in 1990.

"I'm very proud of what I've been able to accomplish in my career and in my life," Nicklaus said.